LUTHER, MÜNZER AND THE BOOKKEEPERS OF THE REFORMATION

by Dieter Forte

translated by Christopher Holme

McGRAW HILL BOOK COMPANY
New York St. Louis San Francisco Toronto

First edition

123456789BPBP79876543

Original edition: *Martin Luther & Thomas Münzer oder Die Einführung der
Buchhaltung* © 1971 Klaus Wagenbach Verlag, Berlin.

All inquiries concerning performance rights in the United States and Canada should
be directed to Miss Toby Cole, 234 West 44th Street, N.Y., N.Y. Telephone:
BR-97770.

Library of Congress Cataloging in Publication Data
Forte, Dieter, Date
Luther, Munzer, and the bookkeeppers of the Reformation.
A play. Translation of Martin Luther und Thomas Münzer.
1. Reformation—Drama.   I. Title.
PT2666.074M313   832'.9'14   72-10074
ISBN 0-07-073776-2
Designed by HELGA MAASS

The practical application to the present makes the understanding of the text very much easier.

—*Martin Luther*

Germans usually can tell you more about Indians than about Germans.

—*Sebastian Franck, Chronica, 1531*

It ill becomes a democratic society in this day and age that it should still see in insurgent peasants nothing but mutinous hordes who were quickly tamed and put in their places by authority. That is how the victors wrote history. It is time for a freedom-loving democratic Germany to write our history differently, and see that it reaches our schoolbooks. I believe we have an unappreciated wealth of events which deserve to be brought to light and to be anchored much more firmly than hitherto in the consciousness of our people. There is nothing to prevent us tracking down in our history and doing justice to those forces which have lived and fought to enable the German people in all political maturity and moral responsibility to mold their own lives and their own order.

—*West German Federal President*
Gustav Heinemann, 1970

THE CHARACTERS:

LUTHER, *34*
MELANCHTHON, *20*
KARLSTADT, *37*
MÜNZER, *27*
FREDERICK OF SAXONY, *54*
His FOOL, *a midget*
SPALATIN, *33, his confidential secretary*
CHARLES V, *19*
MARGARET, *39, his aunt*
GATTINARA, *54, his chancellor*
THE POPE, *46*
CAJETAN, *48, cardinal legate*
FUGGER, *58*
SCHWARZ, *20, his bookkeeper*
ALBERT OF BRANDENBURG, *27*
THE EMPEROR MAXIMILIAN, *60*
BIBBIENA, *51, cardinal*
MILTITZ, *27, diplomat*
FEILITZSCH, *30, counselor*
HUTTEN, *31*
BERLEPSCH, *57, captain*
PFEIFFER, *25*
ERASMUS, *58*
PARACELSUS, *32*
HOLBEIN, *26*
FROBENIUS, *65*
COUNSELORS, CARDINALS, PRINCES, NOBLES, FOOTMEN,
STUDENTS, COMMONERS

Secondary parts can be doubled; the part of the Pope can be played also by a woman.

In the center of the stage right and left, two wooden platforms, each with its own flight of steps.

At the footlights right and left two tables, each with chairs. The actors remain onstage during the performance. *Off* means merely that the actors leave the place where they happen to be playing.

The texts are for the most part in the original words. Figures and facts are accurate.
All currencies have been turned into modern Deutschmarks.

One

"THE WORD OF GOD"

CHORUS   *(several times)*
> When Adam delved and Eve span
> Who was then the gentleman?

(The curtain rises. MÜNZER is demonstrating with students. They march from left to right across stage.)

TABLE RIGHT FRONT

(Three CITIZENS sit at table behind their beer mugs)

1ST CITIZEN   There goes that Münzer again.
2ND CITIZEN   Where he goes, there is trouble.
3RD CITIZEN   Always hanging out with the students.
1ST CITIZEN   They say the town council's corrupt.
3RD CITIZEN   The town council was always corrupt. That means nothing.
CHORUS
> When Adam delved and Eve span
> Who was then the gentleman?

2ND CITIZEN   *(calling out)* And the University will stay shut for good, eh?
3RD CITIZEN   Pretty state of affairs.
4TH CITIZEN   *(entering)* The town council has resigned.
1ST CITIZEN   Just because of Münzer?
2ND CITIZEN   *(calling out)* That'll cost money. Our money it's costing. Do you even have any money?
3RD CITIZEN   Only the man who has money can have an opinion, because then we know his opinion's right.
1ST CITIZEN   Nothing talks better than money. What do I want with opinions?
CHORUS
> When Adam delved and Eve span
> Who was then the gentleman?

(The STUDENTS go off, the CITIZENS follow them.)

PLATFORM RIGHT

(FUGGER kneels at a prie-dieu, a rosary in his folded hands.

SCHWARZ *stands at a high desk on which is a fat book. The Fugger accounts.*)

FUGGER   The beginning.

SCHWARZ   Total capital of the firm Jacob Fugger 19,679,100.

FUGGER   *(crossing himself)* Praise be to Jesus Christ.

SCHWARZ   For ever and ever, Amen. If I as your bookkeeper may be allowed to remark, you are the richest man in Europe.

FUGGER   The business.

SCHWARZ   Albert of Brandenburg.

(ALBERT *comes onto the platform and waits*)

FUGGER   *(sunk in prayer)* Why Mainz?

ALBERT   I want it, and it's available.

FUGGER   The largest and richest see in Germany.

ALBERT   I would accept that into the bargain.

FUGGER   The Church forbids accumulation of offices.

ALBERT   The Church forbids a lot.

FUGGER   You are too young for the office of bishop.

ALBERT   I am archbishop of Magdeburg and administrator of Halberstadt.

FUGGER   And want to be archbishop of Mainz on top of that?

ALBERT   I assume it's a question of money.

FUGGER   Have you money?

ALBERT   Would I be here otherwise?

FUGGER   Schwarz.

SCHWARZ   The archbishopric of Mainz costs in regular fees 1,400,000. To that must be added a bribe for the Holy Father.

ALBERT   Bribe? God forbid!

FUGGER   *(to Schwarz)* A douceur.

SCHWARZ   The Holy Father had in mind a *douceur* of 1,200,000.

ALBERT   Talk of charity!

SCHWARZ   The Holy Father had in mind the Twelve Apostles. 100,000 per head.

ALBERT   Were there really twelve? Isn't the Holy Father making a mistake?

FUGGER   In matters of money the Pope is infallible.

ALBERT   Let's call it 700,000, after the seven mortal sins.

FUGGER   Let's call it a million, after the Ten Commandments, and you have a bargain.

ALBERT   That would be 2,400,000.

FUGGER   Three million.

ALBERT   Ten and fourteen are twenty-four.

FUGGER   The Emperor Maximilian wants something too. It's usual. And the House of Fugger, I regret to say, cannot give its services for nothing.

ALBERT   Three million?

FUGGER   Saxony's very interested.

ALBERT   Twenty-eight.

FUGGER   Twenty-nine.

ALBERT   So be it.

FUGGER   How will you pay?

(ALBERT *shrugs his shoulders*)

SCHWARZ   Mainz is a rich city.

ALBERT   Which has lost three archbishops in succession.

FUGGER   Impoverished therefore.

SCHWARZ   The Lord Archbishop takes over, in Mainz itself, a well-appointed brothel.

ALBERT   I ask you, who goes to the whorehouse any more, when you can get it everywhere for nothing? Business is rapidly falling off.

FUGGER   The Holy Father in his wisdom has foreseen that, and in his exceeding goodness permits us to issue a new loan, the St. Peter's Cathedral indulgence, and appoint you indulgence commissioner.

ALBERT   As I said, a question of money.

FUGGER   Schwarz.

SCHWARZ   Duration eight years. Fifty per cent of the takings to the Holy Father, fifty per cent to the indulgence commissioner.

ALBERT   Sounds possible.

FUGGER   I should mention that the fifty per cent for the Holy Father is not to be set off against the Mainz fees.

ALBERT   Not?

FUGGER   And the other half I, with your permission, shall take on account until your debt to me has been paid off. For this purpose my people will accompany your representatives. They will have a key to every cash box and be cashiers of all the money put in them.

ALBERT   And what do I get?

FUGGER   You get Mainz. *(He gets up from the prie-dieu)* If I may advise you, take Tetzel. First-class man. A great deal of experience. And one more thing. The market at the moment is in an unhealthy state. Prices have dropped badly. So make your offer competitive. Use dynamic salesmanship. There's nothing more to be got out of the usual salvation techniques. Sell indulgences for the dead as well as the living.

ALBERT   Is that allowed?

FUGGER   It isn't allowed, but it can be done. And sell them also to those who don't repent.

ALBERT   Can that be done?

FUGGER   It can't be done, but it's possible. Above all, it brings in business.

ALBERT   I understand nothing of theological matters.

FUGGER   It's enough to have a good bank.

SCHWARZ   We have a large investment section which watches every movement on the indulgence market and keeps our customers informed as a matter of priority.

ALBERT   Where may I sell them?

FUGGER   Not in Saxony.

ALBERT   Without Saxony it's not worth while.

FUGGER   Not in Saxony. Frederick has his own indulgences, and he'll be enough put out by this Mainz affair as it is.

ALBERT   One should have mines.

FUGGER   But you're collecting bishoprics.

(All three leave the platform)

PLATFORM LEFT

(FREDERICK is sitting in an armchair gnawing at a chicken. Behind him at a table FEILITZSCH and a CLERK with lists. On a stand a map.)

FEILITZSCH   (reading out from a register of relics) One piece of the town in which the Virgin Mary was born. One piece of the thread she spun. Two pieces of the chamber in which Mary was greeted by the Angel. One piece of the tree under which Mary conceived the Lord in the Garden of Balm.

FREDERICK   One or two pieces?

FEILITZSCH   One piece.

FREDERICK   Buy a companion piece.

FEILITZSCH   *(reading on)* Four pieces of Mary's shift. Two pieces of Mary's veil which was spattered with blood beneath the cross. One piece of the wax that Mary gave to a worshiping matron.

(SPALATIN *comes onto the platform.* FEILITZSCH, *lowering his voice, reads on*)

FREDERICK   Spalatin, I am vexed.

SPALATIN   What are we to do, Your Electoral Grace? Tetzel has set himself up just across the frontier and the people are running to him in droves. We can't just arrest them.

FREDERICK   I told Fugger: no Saxon money for Albert. I'm not buying bishoprics for that priest's booby. My subjects' money belongs in my pocket. I do owe my people that.

SPALATIN   Formally, everything's in order, Your Electoral Grace. Tetzel hasn't set foot in Saxony.

FREDERICK   Just peddling bits of paper at the frontier. *(He continues gnawing)*

FEILITZSCH   *(reading on with raised voice)* Thirteen pieces of Jesus' crib. A piece of the cloth in which He was swaddled. Two pieces of the hay. A piece of the stone on which Jesus stood in Jerusalem and said, "Here is the center of the world." A piece of the stone on which Jesus was standing when he wept over Jerusalem.

FREDERICK   *(turning around in anguish)* You'll be weeping too, but not over Jerusalem—over Wittenberg, if there's no more money coming in. How am I to sell my reliquary indulgences now? What will All Saints' Day be like in the church of my castle? Who will buy there if he's already bought from Tetzel?

SPALATIN   Undoubtedly business will slacken off considerably.

FREDERICK   Undoubtedly. Fine lot of counselors I've got. *(He starts gnawing again)*

FEILITZSCH   *(continues reading aloud)* A piece of the field of blood which was bought with the thirty pieces of silver for which Christ was betrayed. A piece of the earth on which the Lord sweated drops of blood. (FREDERICK *nods approval*) A piece of the corporal who was spattered with Christ's blood.

FREDERICK   What does this Albert want? What's behind it all? First Magdeburg, then Halberstadt, now Mainz. All territories which once belonged to us. All Saxony is encircled. Brandenburgers planted everywhere. It gives me claustrophobia just to look at the map.

SPALATIN   The Emperor Maximilian. Saxony's too powerful for him. He wants to cut it down to size. If Your Electoral Grace doesn't do something quickly, he *will* cut it down. *(Standing in front of the map)* A further expansion of territory even now would present great difficulties.

FREDERICK   Saxony is the greatest power in Germany.

SPALATIN   But Brandenburg is moving up. They already have two votes in the Electoral College, and they're well aware of the Emperor's plans.

FREDERICK   *(putting away the chicken)* I've got no taste for it any more. *(He stands up, roars)* Am I Frederick of Saxony or am I some two-bit little count? I am the First Prince of Germany and intend to remain so. *(He looks at the map)* Turn away the map. It makes me sick. (SPALATIN *turns the map back to front.* FREDERICK *remains standing before* FEILITSCH)

FEILITZSCH*(reading on)*   Three pieces of the sweatband with which the Lord Jesus' eyes were bound. A piece of the wax of a candle touched by Christ's sweatband. A piece of the wedge with which the cross of Christ was made fast among the stones.

FREDERICK   And my relics? Have they become nothing but rubbish? Why did I invest my money in relics? *(He comes forward again)* It's a complete humbug what Tetzel's doing there. Financial trickery. He's simply selling Fugger's IOUs. Printed paper. Utterly worthless. Just promises. And they call it investment advice. I offer people security. Every indulgence certificate is backed by my relics. Safer than gold. But my good sound reliquary indulgence lies unsold while there's a mad rush for those worthless bits of paper. It's high time we opened the people's eyes.

SPALATIN   It's become such a cutthroat business. The Tetzel representatives go into people's houses and talk them into it. We sit in the church of our castle and wait for the people to come to us.

FREDERICK   I can't be sending my relics here, there, and everywhere.

SPALATIN   Then we must make ourselves more competitive. Still more relics, still more indulgences!

FREDERICK   I never stop buying. How many have we got?

FEILITZSCH   17,443 relics.

SPALATIN   Above all we need more indulgences. We now have 127,799 years and 116 days. That's too few. It must be increased.

FREDERICK   The Pope's still giving out indulgences, but apparently he prefers giving them to others.

SPALATIN   *Douceurs.*

FREDERICK   I've been trying for years. He won't take them.

SPALATIN   Still greater *douceurs.*

FREDERICK   I want to earn money, not spend it. We must open the people's eyes! In Denmark a monk has been preaching against these financial quacks—with success.

SPALATIN   In Germany too there are experts who have spoken about it. Johann von Wesel, Wessel Ganzfort.

FREDERICK   Where are they to be found?

SPALATIN   Dead, I'm afraid.

FREDERICK   Thanks.

SPALATIN   Erasmus of Rotterdam. Your Electoral Grace will find nothing better. The most famous pen in Europe. The Lamp of Learning.

FREDERICK   The Lamp of Learning is too unreliable, I find. You offer to make him a count, and he tells you three times he'll think about it.

SPALATIN   He is independent.

FREDERICK   And here? Is there nothing doing here? Why did I found a university? They suck me dry and we hear nothing of it. What are the professors doing, playing cards?

SPALATIN   Johann von Wesel taught in Erfurt, and we have professors who studied in Erfurt.

FREDERICK   Then let them get on with it. What do I pay these gentlemen for? To discuss the Immaculate Conception? They must concoct something. But quickly. There's no time to be lost. (SPALATIN *goes off.* FREDERICK *sits down again and gnaws his chicken bone*)

FEILITZSCH *(reading on)*   Eight whole thorns from the crown of the
   Lord Jesus. A large piece of the nail which was driven through the
   hand or foot of the Lord Jesus. A reliquary with 178 pieces of
   saints' bones which, since the writing has faded and can no longer
   be read, cannot be listed in detail.
FREDERICK   Shoving his finger into my stew. With my money. I'll
   show that sniveling hound. I'll ram this chicken bone up his arse,
   and then he can hang all his bishop's mitres on it.

(His COURT FOOL, *a midget, has come onto the platform. He
takes the chicken bone away from* FREDERICK, *holds it aloft,
and cries:)*

Part of Saint Frederick's buttock!
(FREDERICK *gives a rumbling laugh*)

TABLE LEFT FRONT

SPALATIN   Dr. Luther! What a coincidence. I was just wondering
   to myself what had become of our Dr. Luther. We hear nothing
   of him.
LUTHER   What should you hear of me? I give lectures. I'm dean of
   studies, vicar of my order, prior of eleven monasteries, administrator of our fishponds, advocate in Torgau, and write the whole
   day long—letters, letters, letters. I could employ two secretaries.
SPALATIN   No time then for theses and disputations?
LUTHER   What about?
SPALATIN   Professors must war with one another. If nothing is
   heard of them, they end by being considered superfluous.
LUTHER   I have published a polemic against scholastic theology. I
   sent it around. I wanted disputations. Nobody answered. Not
   a murmur. And they were sharp theses.
SPALATIN   The University is still young. It hasn't much standing,
   but that can change. Weren't you a student at Erfurt?
LUTHER   Yes.
SPALATIN   Then you certainly know the writings of Johann von
   Wesel.
LUTHER   Of course.

SPALATIN   Including those about indulgences?

LUTHER   Including those.

SPALATIN   Does he write interestingly?

LUTHER   He is against the Pope, against the veneration of saints, the confession, the Holy Communion, the Extreme Unction, the fasts. Pope and councils can err. That sort of thing.

SPALATIN   And against the indulgences?

LUTHER   Why do you ask?

SPALATIN   There is some interest in the question.

LUTHER   At court?

SPALATIN   Have you heard anything about this new indulgence?

LUTHER   The thing is utterly and completely abominable. Tetzel is preaching things that are quite monstrous. The people are being cheated of their salvation.

SPALATIN   Yes, it's bad. And what has the expert to say?

LUTHER   I have drafted some theses——

SPALATIN   Theses? You mean against the indulgence?

LUTHER   Against the abuses to which it is put. There is no objection to the indulgence.

SPALATIN   But why don't we hear about them? This is of the highest interest.

LUTHER   Wesel died at the hands of the Inquisition.

SPALATIN   But . . . that's a long time ago. Those times are past.

LUTHER   The Inquisition is in the hands of the Dominicans, and Tetzel is a Dominican.

SPALATIN   The Elector is not a Dominican.

LUTHER   The theses are incomplete, written off the end of my pen.

SPALATIN   Complete them. Perhaps adding a few sentences about the good German money which in this unjust fashion is flowing to Rome, to fill the Pope's pockets.

LUTHER   What do you need it for?

SPALATIN   Oh well, you know . . . the Elector does like to hear something of his professors occasionally. That's how it is. And you perhaps, is there anything you need?

LUTHER   I could do with a new cowl.

SPALATIN   A new cowl. That can be arranged.

(SPALATIN *goes off.* LUTHER *sits down at the table, strewn*

*with books, and writes. KARLSTADT comes, some books
under his arm. He throws the books on the table and sits down
at the table)*

KARLSTADT   Slavedrivers, curse them.

LUTHER   You're much too kind, Karlstadt.

KARLSTADT   German professor—what a life. And in this miserable
hole too, this hick university.

LUTHER   It would be better if we hadn't so many students here. This
way there can only be disturbances. The Prince ought to take
firm measures.

KARLSTADT   The Prince.

LUTHER   No morals or decency any more. Instead of learning they
run around with girls and ask you silly questions in the bargain.
No proper order. Yesterday one of them asked me where God was
before the creation of the world. I gave him a piece of my mind,
I can tell you.

KARLSTADT   And where was He?

LUTHER   Who?

KARLSTADT   God. (LUTHER *turns to continue his writing*) The
things we preach day after day. We don't believe them. The students don't believe them. The rich don't care, the poor don't know
any better, and the princes like it. And what's it all for? For a
salary. Makes me sick.

LUTHER   The universities ought to be reduced to rubble, the whole
lot of them. They only corrupt the youth. Hotbeds of unbelief
and criticism, all of them. There's nothing in the world reeks
more of hell and the devil than a university.

KARLSTADT   But, my dear fellow, they support their professors.

LUTHER   That's true. Where's that book of yours with the theses
against indulgences?

KARLSTADT   *(hunting a book and reading out the title)* 151 Theses
of Dr. Andreas Karlstadt, Professor of Theology at the University
in Wittenberg. (He throws the book over to LUTHER) Not a soul
took any notice of it. Who does take any interest in such things?

LUTHER   The University is still young. It hasn't much standing. But
that can change.

KARLSTADT   What's that you're writing?
LUTHER   An opinion for the court.

PLATFORM LEFT

(FREDERICK *in an armchair.* SPALATIN *comes up with a sheet of paper in his hand.*)

SPALATIN   The polemic against the indulgences.
FREDERICK   Any good?
SPALATIN   A bit wrong-headed, but usable. If Your Electoral Grace would just glance——
FREDERICK   I don't want to see it. Not one word of it. Want to have nothing to do with it. What I don't know I don't have to disavow. I rely entirely on you in this business. Who wrote it?
SPALATIN   A certain Luther. You once paid for him to take his doctorate. Do you want to see him?
FREDERICK   Never. A good man?
SPALATIN   No fool, but a bit simple.
FREDERICK   Useful therefore. Reliable?
SPALATIN   I think so.
FREDERICK   That's the right mixture. What's his price?
SPALATIN   A new cowl.
FREDERICK   Cheap.
SPALATIN   How should we proceed?
FREDERICK   Let him send it to Albert. And you see that it gets around.

(SPALATIN *goes off*)

TABLE LEFT FRONT

SPALATIN   My dear Luther, your theses have aroused great interest. You may send them to Albert.
LUTHER   To the Archbishop?
SPALATIN   Here is a draft of the letter.
LUTHER   But my good Spalatin! These are theses. Polemical propositions for a scholarly disputation. Something for professors.

SPALATIN   Even princes dispute occasionally.

LUTHER   I don't want our gracious Prince and Albert . . . you understand.

SPALATIN   No I don't.

LUTHER   Two Electors with different viewpoints—politics. What business have my theses there? They could be misunderstood.

SPALATIN   I don't think so.

LUTHER   The Archbishop is my lord and master.

SPALATIN   The Elector is your lord and master. Always the one who pays. *(He hands back the theses)* And try to get Tetzel over here.

LUTHER   What for?

SPALATIN   A little scholarly disputation.

LUTHER   We'll hardly get him to come.

SPALATIN   Safe conduct, food and lodging guaranteed.

LUTHER   By whom? Not by our gracious lord and master?

SPALATIN   By his very self. *(He goes off. LUTHER remains behind, perplexed)*

TABLE RIGHT FRONT

(An OFFICIAL with letters. ALBERT comes on with a PROSTI-TUTE on his arm.)

ALBERT   Well, what do you say? A real child of Mainz.

OFFICIAL   As usual, Your Right Reverend Excellency has picked well.

ALBERT   Anything important?

OFFICIAL   A letter from an Augustinian monk. He complains of the manner in which Tetzel sells his indulgences.

ALBERT   Not important.

OFFICIAL   The letter uses strong language.

ALBERT   Doesn't worry me. We've got other things to think about, eh, my child?

OFFICIAL   The man is a professor at Wittenberg University.

ALBERT   Wittenberg, is there a university there? *(Light dawns on him)* Wittenberg?

OFFICIAL   That's it, Your Excellency.

ALBERT   Frederick. The swine.

PROSTITUTE   But, honey! Is an Archbishop allowed to use words like that?

ALBERT   Only an Archbishop, my child. Only an Archbishop.

OFFICIAL   How will it please Your Right Reverend Excellency to handle the matter?

ALBERT   Let it lie, let it lie, too hot to handle. And at once inform Rome. The Pope will be delighted.

OFFICIAL   Very good, Your Grace.

ALBERT   And now, my child, I'll show you my cathedral.

(They go off laughing. OFFICIAL goes off)

PLATFORM RIGHT

(CARDINAL CAJETAN is reading a book. CARDINAL BIB-BIENA and a SECOND CARDINAL, with books and papers in his hand, come onto the platform.)

BIBBIENA   Ikeymo ith thtanding in front of a church. Reubie, what thort of a houth ith that with the high tower? Ikeymo, that'th a church. What'th a church? Why the goyth thay, that'th where the dear God liveth. But Reubie, the dear God liveth in Heaven. Right, He liveth in Heaven, but in there ith where He hath Hith shop. *(Both laugh)* The Holy Father.

(THE POPE comes onto the platform. He is wearing boots and a long chain about his neck)

POPE   I've shortened my skirt. How do you like the new length?

BIBBIENA   Your Holiness gets freer every day.

CAJETAN   Perhaps we should call a council to fix the skirt length once and for all.

POPE   You would plunge humanity in disaster. There are only two decent topics. The weather and the skirt length. Are we to talk about nothing but the weather?

2nd CARDINAL   If I may draw Your Holiness's attention to the fact, Your Holiness is wearing boots.

POPE   Don't they suit me?

2nd CARDINAL   Your Holiness's feet can no longer be kissed.

POPE   Abolish foot-kissing. *(To* CAJETAN) Are you still studying your Copernicus? The earth turns on itself and turns about the sun.

CAJETAN   He's right.

POPE   I've no objection. I find it nice. So lively. Everything moves. When I think of myself sitting here in the Vatican and rushing through space—nice, I like it.

CAJETAN   The earth is not the center of the world.

POPE   I know. That's Leonardo's opinion, too.

2nd CARDINAL   And so the Pope's not the center of the earth.

POPE   So much for him.

CAJETAN   But when up and down are abolished, what then? Where's Heaven? Where's God?

POPE   Yes, where's God? Bibbiena, you should know that; you're an atheist.

BIBBIENA   You'll find that in my next play.

POPE   Are you writing something new for us?

BIBBIENA   I'm working on a piece in which the most important man hasn't at all a big part but only appears in a short scene at the end.

POPE *(to the* 2ND CARDINAL)   Has Eramus written?

2nd CARDINAL   I'm afraid not.

POPE   Erasmus, there's a man for you. Such education. Such knowledge. Such style. But he won't come. All he does is take money.

CAJETAN   A writer.

BIBBIENA   Make him a cardinal.

POPE   A good idea. I'll make only artists, scholars, and atheists cardinals in future. There's the complete solution. All priests to be excommunicated and the lap of Holy Church transferred to her head. . . . What is there?

2nd CARDINAL   A report on the Holy Inquisition in Spain, which doesn't seem to be all that holy.

POPE   Are they still at it? No, that I will not have. Such pettiness. Every day the world gets larger and wider. America, Africa, India, China. Everywhere new countries, new peoples, and everywhere old civilizations, old religions. Such bigotry! We're not the only ones. One religion among many. Nobody's entirely in the right. This fable of the Christ, goodness yes, it brings in money. I'm just reading Plato. There's a man I prefer.

CAJETAN   I can recommend the Koran to your holiness.

POPE   One can only learn. That's all. My doctor's a Jew. One of my best friends is a Moor. You know Al-Hasan ibn Muhammad al-Wazzan? He's traveled over half Africa. He's writing a book about it. What civilization, what things of beauty! They have civilizations there which are thousands of years older than ours. Stupid niggers forsooth! A story the merchants tell us so that they can sell them as slaves. I'm strictly against it. And the Indians too across the Atlantic. I'm against their being enslaved. I will not permit that. We must issue a bull or something. Remind me about it. . . . Anything else?

2nd CARDINAL *(giving the POPE a book)*   The Talmud.

POPE   Oh, splendid. I've had the Talmud printed. There was no printed edition before. A scandal. *(To BIBBIENA)* Look, the binding.

2nd CARDINAL   Morocco.

POPE   And the print.

2nd CARDINAL   Black-letter.

BIBBIENA   *(observing the POPE'S chain)* A new chain?

POPE   Cellini. By the way, Cellini's having a private opening. We must go to it. *(To CAJETAN)* Have you seen Raphael's pictures? He's decorated Bibbiena's bathroom. As Pope, I can tell you it makes me blush.

CAJETAN   I prefer Leonardo da Vinci.

POPE   Leonardo's a genius, I know. But he never follows anything to the end. All just ideas. A game of concepts.

BIBBIENA   The *Mona Lisa's* magnificent.

POPE   The *Mona Lisa's* good. But he hardly paints any more. The other day he staged another of his happenings. He locked the people in a room with a pile of cleaned sheep's intestines. Then from a neighboring room he blew up the intestines with bellows until everybody was pressed against the wall. In this way they'd see the air, he said.

2ND CARDINAL   These modern artists!

BIBBIENA   Titian came to see me. He wanted an advance.

POPE   Do you think Titian's good?

CAJETAN   Michelangelo for me.

POPE   Ah, Michelangelo.

CAJETAN   The greatest genius of the lot. I was in his workshop.

POPE   I confess, those ceiling paintings in the Sistine Chapel, they bowl you over. All the same, I'm a Raphael enthusiast. The plans for St. Peter's. What a building that'll be! But it will cost millions. I've just issued another indulgence on it.

2ND CARDINAL   Indulgence. There's some agitation in Germany. A professor is protesting against the St. Peter's indulgence.

POPE   Send him Raphael's designs.

2ND CARDINAL   Frederick of Saxony is probably behind it.

POPE   Oh, him! He's another; he only wants indulgences. Give him some. That'll do the trick. Write to him that a whole shipload of relics has just come in, of particles of the Holy Cross, bones of various saints, and the little hankies of baby Jesus. Tell him to be quick and lay in a stock.

2ND CARDINAL   The Portuguese ambassador would like to present Your Holiness with a white elephant.

POPE   A white elephant? A miracle of God.

PLATFORM LEFT

(FEILITSCH *is showing* FREDERICK *some new relics.*)

FEILITZSCH   An armbone of St. Benno.

FREDERICK   Fine piece. Splendid. And just the length of mine.

(SPALATIN *comes onto the platform*)

FEILITZSCH   A comb of St. Ursula with seventeen hairs.

FREDERICK   Charming. *(To* SPALATIN*)* The newest relics for the Frankfurt Fair.

SPALATIN   I've seen the bill.

FREDERICK   The price doesn't matter. Quality. Quality. If the people are to shuffle through the church on their knees they must be offered something. One must never cheat the people, eh, Spalatin?

SPALATIN   Never, Your Electoral Grace.

FREDERICK   Quality always pays.

FEILITZSCH   A bottle of the milk of the Holy Virgin Mary.

FREDERICK   Delicious. Delicious. A real find. How many bottles have we got now?

FEILITZSCH   Five.

FREDERICK   Genuine?

FEILITZSCH   Certificates of the most famous universities of Paris and Basel are available. It seems that it's a very early milk. Ten days after birth.

FREDERICK   The century of science. It's a pleasure to be alive. What do you say to today's post, Spalatin? The Pope is sending new indulgences. We shall earn a great deal, a very great deal of money. The affair looks really better than I thought. The man shall have his cowl.

SPALATIN   In many towns the aristocracy is supporting the dissemination of the theses.

FREDERICK   No doubt they are.

SPALATIN   The people's reaction too has been very positive.

FREDERICK   There you see again. We're always underestimating the people.

SPALATIN   Now Your Electoral Grace is letting his goodness of heart run away with him.

FREDERICK   I know, I know. And so that the Pope may know how the people think, let this fellow send his theses to Rome. A nice covering letter, a little bit diplomatic, but you write that for him. Altogether, it would be good if you kept an eye on his work. To keep him on the right lines.

SPALATIN   He shows me everything he writes.

FREDERICK   That's the way. Do you think he can manage it— quite on his own like that?

SPALATIN   One must wait and see.

FREDERICK   That's not sure enough for me. Who else have we got?

SPALATIN   Karlstadt.

FREDERICK   Any good?

SPALATIN   A radical mind.

FREDERICK   Perhaps we should look for reinforcements.

SPALATIN   If it gets serious we need a man to make sure of Luther's scholarship, one who knows Greek and Hebrew.

FREDERICK   Have you got someone?

SPALATIN   Melanchthon. Still very young, but an extremely intelligent fellow.

FREDERICK   Get him here. We need these young people now. A bit of revolutionary spirit does no harm. We live in unsettled times.

Everything's in a state of upheaval. No time to be niggardly with intelligence. Besides, it's cheap.

SPALATIN   It's natural for the young people to have their worries.

FREDERICK   Tell them they're under my electoral protection. Nothing will happen to them. They're our dear young people on whom we shall keep a gracious eye. And make it clear to Luther he must be steadfast. We have great hopes of his steadfastness. Have you got the papers for the Augsburg Diet?

SPALATIN   In the closet.

FREDERICK   We must be thoroughly prepared. (Taking the milk bottle in his hand) Really genuine?

FEILITZSCH   Certificates from—

FREDERICK   I know, I know. (He sniffs at the bottle, then takes a sip) Heavenly.

(All go off. Cheerful music. Drinks and snacks are put on the tables. Until the end of the Luther-Cajetan scene an orgy of eating and drinking develops over the whole stage. Left a FOOTMAN. FUGGER comes from behind up to the footlights. GUESTS pour in.)

FUGGER   Gentlemen, I welcome you to the Diet of Augsburg. I hope you are comfortable in my house.

FOOTMAN   (announcing) Cardinal Albert of Brandenburg.

ALBERT   (entering) Cardinal! My dear Fugger, Cardinal!

FUGGER   I congratulate you. When will you be Pope?

ALBERT   A question of money, just a question of money. (He turns around) Does it suit me?

FUGGER   Excellently.

ALBERT   I find it lends a man a touch of godliness.

FUGGER   I'm not sure what God is wearing just now.

ALBERT   You're a heretic, my friend. I'll light your pyre with my own princely hand.

FUGGER   Yes, but please not until you've paid your debts.

ALBERT   A man of figures. From head to foot nothing but figures. Do you sleep with them too?

FUGGER   With the noughts.

ALBERT   Horrible. Talking about noughts. What's on the agenda?

FUGGER   The Emperor Maximilian wants to make Charles his successor.

ALBERT   Well I never! That's new. The little runt from Spain?

FUGGER   Yes.

ALBERT   And so he needs our votes?

FUGGER   Are you in favor of Charles?

ALBERT   I'm in favor of anything I'm paid for.

FUGGER   I'm paying.

ALBERT   For Charles?

FUGGER   *(with a slight bow)* Your Eminence.

ALBERT   One more *Eminence* and I might agree to anything.

FOOTMAN   *(announcing)* The Elector Frederick of Saxony. (FREDERICK *enters*)

ALBERT   Oh, that boor of a Saxon! Where's the wine?

FUGGER   Over there. (*To* FREDERICK) Did you have a good journey?

FREDERICK   Rather a long one. But recently the Diets are held only in your house.

FUGGER   It's come about that way.

FREDERICK   Have you now got a monopoly of Diets?

FUGGER   A dead loss.

FREDERICK   By the way, I owe you an apology. That stupid matter of the indulgences.

FUGGER   But my dear Prince, not at all.

FREDERICK   You had some losses.

FUGGER   Small change. Besides, I was insured. You know, I've long been distrustful of that market. The boom is over. If I may advise you, be cautious about your investment there in the future.

FREDERICK   My relics are still doing well.

FUGGER   Relics will still keep going for a while. There you have something to see. You can believe in them. But this certificate nonsense is dead. How are your mines doing?

FREDERICK   Could be better. A shortage of workmen.

FUGGER   We're stuck in an inflationary boom. A huge demand, and the labor market is cleaned out.

FREDERICK   And the workmen demand higher wages. It wipes out all your profits.

FUGGER   I've just rationalized all through. We're working a new system. Three seven-hour shifts.

FREDERICK   Where do you get the people?

FUGGER   The workmen mustn't get too high wages. Then they work two shifts in a row.

FREDERICK   They'll demand higher wages.

FUGGER   Introduce a wage freeze. Keep wages low and raise prices steeply.

FREDERICK   The workmen will run away.

FUGGER   Forbid anyone to change his place of work. Above all, no employer must take on a workman who has stirred up discontent anywhere else. I recommend the system to you. Your cousin, Duke George, has already introduced it. He is very satisfied. I should be very glad to help you.

FREDERICK   What would your help cost?

FUGGER   Not what you think, Prince. I own the largest and most productive mines in all Europe. The few free mines don't worry me. They're dependent on me in any case. The big profits are not in producing the raw material but in processing it. The metallurgical plant, smelting works, forges, foundries, cannon factories. It's the combination of processes does it. That's where the profit lies. Your mines and your metallurgical plants. if you'll forgive me, they're all still cottage industry.

FREDERICK   Don't forget, your biggest and most modern plant is on my territory and dependent on my protection.

FUGGER   Of which let us hope it is assured for all time.

FREDERICK   Let us hope so. One never knows what might happen. And from this plant you supply Germany, Holland, Spain, and Portugal. Important markets.

FUGGER   My dear Prince. I hold the European monopoly of ore, gold, iron, lead, above all tin, silver, and copper. Of copper actually the world monopoly. My house is the most powerful bank in Europe. I can put my metal into storage for two years. But I can also flood the market. As I please. I can keep the prices high, and you will share the profit of that. But I can also lower the prices, and keep them so low for so long that you will be glad to make me a present of your mines. There are others I've made bankrupt before now. But what kind of talk is this? Look, we two are the only industrialists. You have mines, I have mines. The rest sit over there drinking and have nothing. You know I admire you. A businessman with initiative, who goes his own way. Only, without your mines you won't have any way to go.

FREDERICK   And without your metallurgical plant your combine would lose half its value.

FUGGER   What have you got against my metallurgical plant?

FREDERICK   It lies in my mining territory.

FUGGER   That's a good site.

FREDERICK   But unfortunately it processes almost exclusively your Hungarian ore. Competitors' ore. At prices which make my mine-owers gasp.

FUGGER   I take ore from your territory too. For example, there's a certain Luther, mine-owner, who supplies me, and he they say has a son.

FREDERICK   Yes, so they say. But perhaps this Luther would like to sell more ore at a better price.

FUGGER   If I can increase production, certainly. My dear Prince, we both know that it can't go on like this. We need a new work ethic. Do you know we have over a hundred church feast days a year? Over a hundred holidays, dear Prince. Fairs, pilgrimages, all the lot. The people eat and drink themselves silly and never think of work. If these useless holidays were eliminated, annual production would be increased by a third, profit by a half at least, and the labor-market problem would be solved. And then these fast days. I must be continually applying for exemptions for my workmen. A workman must work, not fast. This must be regulated once and for all. The day's work must be sanctified. The people should thank God merely for being allowed to work. Their wages they can get in Heaven. Then they won't need so much on earth and we will at last have a cheap labor force. Tell that to your Luther.

FREDERICK   To which one?

FUGGER   The father, of course.

FOOTMAN   *(announcing)* The Emperor Maximilian.

MAXIMILIAN   *(entering)* How-do, folks, how-do, sound as a bell I am, I thank ye, sound as a bell. How-do, Fugger. How-do, Frederick. Sound as a bell.

FUGGER   Was it the water did the trick?

MAXIMILIAN   Wonderful. One cup of water, and I'm right as rain.

FREDERICK   Water?

MAXIMILIAN   Plain water, nothin' better. Lookee Fugger, I need coin.

FUGGER   I am at Your Majesty's disposal, in my office. *(Goes off)*

MAXIMILIAN   I'll be with ye in a moment. Eh, Frederick lad, you're lookin' champion. *(He taps him on the belly)* But mind the fried chicken, eh, go careful now!

FREDERICK   Better than a dropsy.

MAXIMILIAN   Ah, now you're makin' fun o' me! Harkee Frederick, you're for Charlie, eh, that's my grandson?

FREDERICK   That we must see.

MAXIMILIAN   Eh, you can't do that to me. Such a fine lad, and so keen to be my successor. Look ye, the Netherlands, Burgundy, and Spain he has already, and half Italy besides and that new— what's it called—America. From me he gets Austria, Hungary. Switzerland I lost—no matter. He'll make up with Bohemia, Moravia, and Silesia. There's nothing now he wants but Germany. Such a pleasure it'd give the lad.

FREDERICK   And France? And the Pope?

MAXIMILIAN   Eh, he'll make short work of them.

FREDERICK   And then he'll make short work of us.

MAXIMILIAN   Eh, shame on you, harborin' such thoughts among kinsfolk! Come now, you'll speak for him?

FREDERICK   What's in it for me?

MAXIMILIAN   I know you're angry I let Albert have Mainz. But what was I to do? Don't matter a bag of beans anyway. But we'll come to an arrangement. If you'll speak for Charlie, my word as Emperor, we'll come to an arrangement.

FREDERICK   First I must come to an arrangement with the Pope.

MAXIMILIAN   Ah, that with Luther there, an excellent stroke. Excellent. A masterpiece. A good lad, and mind ye look well after him. Preserve him with care. A lad like that Luther will have his uses in time to come. I'm thinking the occasion will soon offer that we can employ him. If I had a man like that! But no such brainwave ever comes my way. A few years gone, I tried to turn the German Church into cash. But it didn't come off. The

Pope's rents from Germany are a hundred times what mine are, you know that? A hundred times! That's what I call coin.

FREDERICK   You denounced him to the Pope.

MAXIMILIAN   Policy, policy. What should I do? Cajetan put the letter before me. And so I signed. But that signifies nothin'. All the more important he'll be. That's the cream of the jest. Now it's official. Now he's really got a price; now you can ask good money for him. You haven't by any chance a thousand on you?

FREDERICK   All on deposit with Fugger.

MAXIMILIAN   The way you all give your money to Fugger! A hundred? I'm so broke I drink nothing but water.

FREDERICK   Good for the health.

MAXIMILIAN   Now, now. That's all a fabrication from my press office.

VILLINGER   (coming up to MAXIMILIAN with papers in his hand) Your Majesty.

MAXIMILIAN   What is it? (VILLINGER points to the papers)

MAXIMILIAN   (to FREDERICK) Excuse me a minute, will you? (MAXIMILIAN goes apart with VILLINGER. FREDERICK goes to a table)

VILLINGER   Letters from Charles. He says we should appeal to the claims of kinship.

MAXIMILIAN   Kinship? Has the lad gone crazy? Coin. Loads of it. Nothing else is any use. When you think what the Frenchman has already stuffed into the electors' pockets. They never take their fingers out of the cashbox. Altogether, the things that go on, you wouldn't believe. You can't just hand out bribes. But one way or another, we must give more. The lad's getting rich territories, he mustn't be close-fisted.

VILLINGER   Charles thought four hundred thousand per elector.

MAXIMILIAN   Four hundred thousand. Don't make me laugh. The lad's too good for this world. Four hundred thousand is small change—they'll drink it in an evening. Millions. You just have to keep pouring. Princes, knights, gentlemen, secretaries, all must be well greased. And women must be provided. The Archduke of Brandenburg has been promised the Princess Renee by the Frenchman, so we must give him at least Catharine for his bed, otherwise we shall get nowhere.

VILLINGER   Charles' sister?

MAXIMILIAN   Let her make herself useful for once. Everything must be custom-built. While I remember, the Bavarian won't have Joanna—you know, the one from Naples. Doesn't like the look of her. And yet she's a fine lass. Ah, well, a matter of taste. So let's give him the daughter of that Hernandez. But no more exchanges. And his brother, he's willing too. We'll give him Eleonora as a bedfellow.

VILLINGER   The King of Portugal was to get her.

MAXIMILIAN   He shan't have her. Old bag of bones. Just about suit him, that would. Wouldn't know what to do with her anyway.

VILLINGER   So Catharine—

MAXIMILIAN   —for the Archduke of Brandenburg. That's to say, shouldn't we do better to give her to Frederick's nephew? He's now just at the age, and the Saxon anyway's a bit peevish.

VILLINGER   And an important man.

MAXIMILIAN   The most important. So change it around. Catharine to Saxony. But what'll I give to Brandenburg? It's a teaser. More princes than women. The Swiss. My God, the Swiss! I forgot them. What do we do there? Coin they've got already. What I give them for bedfellows is more than I can tell. A republic! Look into it, Villinger, and then see if you can get that Luther over to us. What good is he doing in Saxony? Austria's much nicer anyway.

FOOTMAN   (announcing) Cardinal Legate Cajetan.

MAXIMILIAN   (calling across) Come over here, Cajetan, more fun here. Come over. (MAXIMILIAN draws FREDERICK to him. CAJETAN comes) Do you know one another?

CAJETAN   No. (A FOOTMAN brings wine in glasses. All three take a glass)

MAXIMILIAN   This is Frederick of Saxony. That's the country which lies—well, pretty far down. (CAJETAN and FREDERICK greet one another)

FREDERICK   How do you like Germany?

CAJETAN   I feel horribly cold. Where do you keep your sun? How can one live without sun?

MAXIMILIAN   Well let me tell you something. I'm Emperor of the whole shooting match. Now then, I'm an Austrian, that's to say still human. But the Germans! Twenty-five years I've been trying to rule them. But they beat me. You'll see what I mean. There are Bavarians and Württembergers and Hessians and Thuringians, people of the Palatinate, Rhinelanders, Brandenburgers, Hamburgers, Lübeckers—

FREDERICK   And Saxons.

MAXIMILIAN   And Saxons. Don't know them all myself. But for waging war, there you can use them. Fantastic. Anywhere the banging starts, you can wager there'll be Germans involved. They'll fight anyone for you. And an endurance they've got, superb. The campaigns I've fought with them. Marvelous. First the artillery, bang bang, and then the Germans. The artillery. There's an invention for you. There I'm an expert. If I could I'd build an artillery that—You haven't by any chance got a thousand on you?

CAJETAN   I'm extremely sorry.

MAXIMILIAN   Can't you give me your ring?

CAJETAN   My ring?

FREDERICK   The pawnbroker's shut.

MAXIMILIAN   That's true too. Yes. How's the Pope?

CAJETAN   His Holiness is in excellent health.

MAXIMILIAN   Pope, that's what one should be, that'd be fine. Nearly was too. But Fugger wouldn't put up the money for me. Pity. Would've been a splendid income, and then I'd have been a saint, and you'd have had to pray to me after my death. On your knees. Would have done me good.

CAJETAN   At least you've saved yourself worry about a German heretic.

MAXIMILIAN   Now see you handle that Luther with care. With great care, eh, Frederick? A very tricky subject.

CAJETAN   I thought it was Your Majesty's opinion that—

MAXIMILIAN   So it is. I was just saying to Frederick, it's time that Luther was burned. Didn't I say that?

FREDERICK   When?

MAXIMILIAN   A moment ago. You know, just after that business about the water, then I said—don't you remember?

FREDERICK   No.

MAXIMILIAN   *(to Cajetan)* He's forgotten. Yes. *(To the* FOOTMAN *as he passes)* You, lad, haven't got a ten-spot on you, eh?

FOOTMAN   No, Your Majesty.

MAXIMILIAN   Ah well, no matter. It's a bad day today. I'll have to go to Fugger. Have a good time, lads. Later we'll have a few drinks.

CAJETAN   Only question is what of.

FREDERICK   A round of water perhaps.

MAXIMILIAN   *(at a table)* How-do, how-do.

(CAJETAN *and* FREDERICK *take stock of each other*)

CAJETAN   Elector?

FREDERICK   Cardinal.

CAJETAN   The Holy Father has recently had some annoyance from one of your countrymen. Annoyance which has already had an appreciable effect on the Holy Father's receipts.

FREDERICK   Theological matters. I never interfere in them. I'm an ignorant layman.

CAJETAN   And a Christian Prince.

FREDERICK   A loyal son of the Roman Church. Ready for any sacrifice.

CAJETAN   The said Luther holds heretical opinions.

FREDERICK   Yes, you must settle that with him personally. As I said, I understand nothing of such things.

CAJETAN   It is quite sufficient if you hand him over to the Church. We shall then look after him until tempers have cooled.

FREDERICK   Hand him over with pleasure, but how?

CAJETAN   Am I not speaking to the Elector of Saxony?

FREDERICK   Yes indeed. But I should first have to see what my subjects have to say about it.

CAJETAN   Oh.

FREDERICK   Yes, it's a business with us here in Germany. We princes can do absolutely nothing. On every little thing we have to consult our subjects.

CAJETAN   Interesting constitutional system. Who is the ruler then among you? The Emperor? The princes? Or the subjects?

FREDERICK   Oh the subjects. And there you have Bavarians, Württemburgers, Hessians, Thuringians, Palatinate folk, Rhinelanders, Hambergers, Brandenburgers,—

CAJETAN   And Saxons.

FREDERICK   And Saxons.

CAJETAN   And supposing I should want to examine a Saxon subject named Luther?

FREDERICK   The best thing is to ask him if he'll come.

CAJETAN   And where shall I find him?

FREDERICK   I think he lives in Wittenberg.

CAJETAN   You think.

FREDERICK   I could of course be mistaken. We have no domiciliary register.

CAJETAN   *(loudly)* Elector.

FREDERICK   Cardinal.

CAJETAN   *(tugging at his collar)* It's warm here.

FREDERICK   A moment ago you were freezing. You see how quickly you get used to the climate. And the climate just now is such that we shall soon have Charles as German Emperor. And that would make Charles lord of all Europe, if we overlook a few odd spots like France and the Vatican.

CAJETAN   A horrifying thought. A catastrophe.

FREDERICK   He's said to be a nice lad.

CAJETAN   The Holy Father is unconditonally opposed to it. Charles for the Holy Father's taste would be much too powerful.

FREDERICK   All the rest meanwhile are for Charles. The Pope's only got me left. What will he pay?

CAJETAN   If you can prevent Charles' election, there's a lot we could discuss.

FREDERICK   How much?

CAJETAN   In that case the Pope would confer on you the Golden Rose of Virtue. The highest decoration of Christendom. And an ornament for your collection. The whole world would pay to see it.

FREDERICK   Indulgences?

CAJETAN   Would without question be awarded you in the most generous fashion.

FREDERICK   Luther?

CAJETAN   Luther could be overlooked. Provided he doesn't engage in any new assaults. One must set bounds somewhere. You understand. The Pope is still after all the Pope.

FREDERICK   Very well.

CAJETAN   You'll vote against Charles?

FREDERICK   And the Pope will keep his promise. Otherwise I'll set Luther on him.

CAJETAN   The idea you have of the Pope!

FREDERICK   Nothing good.

CAJETAN   I didn't know you had a sense of humor.

FREDERICK   That's the dangerous thing about the Germans.

CAJETAN   *(laughing)* But a conversation with your Luther I must have. Why else am I here? But the publicity—it would attract notice.

FREDERICK   You'll examine him here in Augsburg, a fatherly examination, I insist, and then you'll send him back in good health.

CAJETAN   Back to Wittenberg?

FREDERICK   If that's where he wants to go.

CAJETAN   But will he come? Since your subjects are sovereign.

FREDERICK   I shall talk him into it.

CAJETAN   Too kind.

FREDERICK   *(bowing)* Cardinal.

CAJETAN   *(bowing)* Elector. *(He goes to a table)*

FREDERICK   *(nodding SPALATIN over to him)* I'm getting the Golden Rose of Virtue.

SPALATIN   The Rose?

FREDERICK   For which I've waited four years. A bargain, Spalatin. *(He rubs his hands)*

SPALATIN   And Luther?

FREDERICK   Send for him. Give him my best advice. Don't let him out of your sight. Don't let him move one step alone. Everything must be timed exactly. And tell him to be steadfast. If he recants the devil will take him. I'll pay his travel expenses too.

(SPALATIN *goes off.* FREDERICK *goes to table)*

PLATFORM RIGHT

(FUGGER *and* SCHWARZ *at their bookkeeping at a standing desk.* MAXIMILIAN *comes onto the platform.)*

MAXIMILIAN   How-do, how-do, you've a new man?

FUGGER   My chief bookkeeper.

MAXIMILIAN   Ah, librarian. How-do, young feller. What's that fat book you have?

SCHWARZ   It's the double bookkeeping, Your Majesty.

MAXIMILIAN   I'd like one of those; are there pictures in it?

SCHWARZ   Figures, your majesty.

MAXIMILIAN   *(bored)* Oh, figures.

SCHWARZ   It's an art.

MAXIMILIAN   Since when are figures an art?

SCHWARZ   It's the newest thing, Your Majesty.

MAXIMILIAN   What are these artistic figures?

FUGGER   My business transactions.

MAXIMILIAN   But they were always written down.

FUGGER   Now we no longer write anything but money. No wagon-loads or shiploads. Cannon, cloth, flour, wool, copper. Goods, animals, people, all are turned into capital that must increase.

SCHWARZ   And the soul of capital is bookkeeping.

MAXIMILIAN   Who are you foolin'? Frippery!

FUGGER   The greatest invention of man. We are no longer distracted by details. Sentimentalities, consideration for any sort of things or persons. We no longer see anything but money. And money must increase.

MAXIMILIAN   Coin? You have to spend that.

FUGGER   Your Majesty is mistaken: it must increase.

SCHWARZ   With interest and compound interest.

MAXIMILIAN   What, interest twice over on the same money? Heavens, what a pair of rogues! When the Church don't allow interest at all.

FUGGER   Your Majesty is again mistaken. Compound interest. If I—

MAXIMILIAN   Let be, let be, I understand nothin' about it anyway. Rather wage a war any day.

FUGGER   This book decides whether Your Majesty can wage a war.

MAXIMILIAN   What, am I in it too?

SCHWARZ   Your Majesty fills several pages.

MAXIMILIAN   Devil's work.

SCHWARZ   Entirely Christian. Invented by a Franciscan.

MAXIMILIAN   Trust the monks. Lookee, Fugger, I need coin.

FUGGER   Schwarz.

SCHWARZ   Your Majesty is 23,585,400 in deficit.

MAXIMILIAN   In what?

FUGGER   Your Majesty owes us this sum.

MAXIMILIAN   Don't talk to me of old debts. Food that's been eaten.

FUGGER   Your Majesty's account is heavily overdrawn, and in consideration of your age—

MAXIMILIAN   What does that mean?

FUGGER   It means that you will soon die in any case.

MAXIMILIAN   Well, that's a fine way to talk to a man! Is that part of your bookkeeping?

FUGGER   It comes out of it.

MAXIMILIAN   But you've made millions out of me.

FUGGER   That's a different account.

MAXIMILIAN   Transfer it there.

FUGGER   Can't be done.

MAXIMILIAN   You've got the money.

FUGGER   As I said, a different account.

MAXIMILIAN   Give it me from there.

FUGGER   It can only be done through the book and the book demands security.

MAXIMILIAN   But goddammit! What have I left to give you? The whole country belongs to you already, mines, plant, the whole industry. Everything. It's you who pay my officials and my ministers. All I'm left with is a hope they don't laugh at me.

(FUGGER *shrugs his shoulders*)

MAXIMILIAN   *(roaring)* Villinger, Villinger. *(He runs down the steps)*

FUGGER   Have we still got the Innsbruck stuff?

SCHWARZ   From the bankruptcy? They're lying around still. Nobody will take them.

(MAXIMILIAN *comes back onto the platform. He drags* VILLINGER *with him*)

MAXIMILIAN   Come on, come on. *(To* FUGGER) My Chancellor of the Exchequer will stand surety.

FUGGER   I'm afraid that won't do. He's already done so.

MAXIMILIAN   Is that true?

VILLINGER   Yes.

MAXIMILIAN   Well, that's dandy. Here I sit in my Diet—

FUGGER   In *your* Diet? Your Majesty forgets that *I* pay for this Diet.

MAXIMILIAN   *(helplessly)* Villinger.

VILLINGER   Couldn't you at least give His Majesty some pocket money?

MAXIMILIAN   I have to entertain those stupid hicks down there, and I haven't got a crown left.

FUGGER   One hundred thousand.

MAXIMILIAN   What can I do with one hundred thousand. They drink like fishes.

FUGGER   Three hundred thousand.

MAXIMILIAN   There, I knew it. You're human after all. But not with that compound interest clapped on.

FUGGER   Free of interest.

MAXIMILIAN   Fantastic. I tell you, he's human. A man you can talk to.

VILLINGER   The conditions?

FUGGER   The loan will be paid off by ore deliveries. In addition you will buy for one hundred thousand a consignment of ore, first-class goods from my Innsbruck store.

VILLINGER   Your Innsbruck ore has been investigated by our experts. It's completely unusable. Dross.

FUGGER   In addition, for 80,000 a consignment of valuable cloth, also from Innsbruck.

VILLINGER   Thank you. We know that stuff too. It's not cloth. It's rags. Would you offer the Emperor rags and rubble?

FUGGER   Your Majesty can choose.

MAXIMILIAN   Where must I sign? (SCHWARZ *lays a receipt before him.* MAXIMILIAN *is about to sign*)

VILLINGER   May I? *(He picks up the receipt)* Your Majesty is here signing a receipt for 350,000. That's 50,000 more than you're getting. In addition, 180,000 for unsalable goods. So Your Majesty is paying 230,000 to get 300,000, which over and above that has to be paid off by ore deliveries.

MAXIMILIAN   There, you see, and I thought it was a bargain.

(VILLINGER *lays down the receipt and goes off*)

MAXIMILIAN   *(signing)* I think it really would be better if I die soon.

PLATFORM LEFT

(CAJETAN *in an armchair.* LUTHER, FEILITZSCH, *and several counselors ascend the platform.*)

CAJETAN   Where's Luther?

LUTHER   Very Reverend Father.

CAJETAN   And the other gentlemen?

LUTHER   My counselors.

CAJETAN   If the gentlemen would not mind retiring to the hall for a moment. (*The* COUNSELORS *hesitate*) I'm not a cannibal.

(FEILITZSCH *whispers something in* LUTHER's *ear.* LUTHER *nods.* FEILITZSCH *and the* COUNSELORS *leave the platform.* LUTHER *prostates himself*)

CAJETAN   Get up, my son, get up. (LUTHER *gets up but remains kneeling*) But, my son, what's the meaning of this performance? Please get up.

LUTHER   Pardon me, Very Reverend Father. I was so instructed.

CAJETAN   It would have been better to be punctual.

LUTHER   Pardon me, Very Reverend Father, I had to conform to the instructions of the electoral counselors. They wanted an imperial safe conduct. I wasn't even allowed on the street.

CAJETAN   That was all arranged with the Elector. Were you not informed?

LUTHER   I was informed, Very Reverend Father, but am obliged to conform strictly to—

CAJETAN   —the instructions of the electoral counselors. Yes, your Elector is very concerned about you.

LUTHER   I don't understand, Very Reverend Father.

CAJETAN   Well then, listen, my son. We are neither of us in a very pleasant position, and before having our official interview we can perhaps have a sensible talk. You discovered irregularities in the indulgence trade—

LUTHER   Pardon me, Very Reverend Father, for interrupting you. That's not so.

CAJETAN   What?

LUTHER   Acquaintances came to me in indignation at the manner in which the indulgences were being sold. I tried to avoid being drawn in, but it came to statements which actually endangered the good repute of the Pope.

CAJETAN   How dreadful.

LUTHER   What was I to do? I didn't at all want to oppose the indulgence-sellers. Indeed, I wished with all my heart that their sermons could seem to everyone the pure truth. It was others who had reasons against the indulgences; they talked me into it so insistently that I was finally cornered.

CAJETAN   But you did write it?

LUTHER   Yes, I did, but all I wanted was a disputation. I thought that would be the best way out, because I wanted to agree with nobody and to contradict nobody. It was far from my intention to cause the Pope any annoyance.

CAJETAN   Far from yours, perhaps.

LUTHER   I don't understand, Very Reverend Father.

CAJETAN   That seems usual here.

LUTHER   I don't understand that either, Very Reverend Father.

CAJETAN   Now listen, my son, you're making much too much of all this. Very well, wrong things have been preached, much was not right, but what does that signify? The important thing is that there should be money coming in.

LUTHER   And the souls of the faithful?

CAJETAN   The indulgences are a tax, an offering, nothing more. The Church lives on them, the princes, all of us, and you too are paid from them, and it must come from somewhere.

LUTHER   But the souls of the faithful?

CAJETAN   We're talking about money. Even your Christian Elector that time simply kept the Turkish war indulgences and built your university with it.

LUTHER   Because you wage no war against the Turks.

CAJETAN   Would you reproach the Pope for *not* waging war?

LUTHER   What would the Pope say if the Sultan marched into Rome?

CAJETAN   The Holy Father is a polite man. He will wish him good day.

LUTHER   You're making fun of me.

CAJETAN My dear son, again you're taking things too seriously. You Germans are terrible. Look, the Turks are very nice people. The Sultan is an honorable man. We get on very well with one another. We do business, earn money. A livelihood for everyone.

LUTHER The Sultan wants to conquer Europe.

CAJETAN Oh, goodness. That's all been settled. There are verbal arrangements.

LUTHER And if the Sultan doesn't respect them?

CAJETAN Then we'll become Mohammedans. Very interesting religion.

LUTHER Why is the Pope collecting money then?

CAJETAN The artists. You can't imagine what it's like. Nothing but advances the whole time.

LUTHER Why then for the Turkish war?

CAJETAN Do you think the people will give money if the Pope has nothing to say but "I must pay my artists"? They'll only give if they're provided with a mortal enemy. They must be afraid of Them over There, afraid that They'll come over Here and that they themselves will be worse off for it. Otherwise nobody will pay. If the Pope is honest and says "I want to build St. Peter's," someone like you is sure to come squawking— What's that about St. Peter's? (Pause) And yet it's going to be a marvelous thing. First Michelangelo is to—

LUTHER Who's Michelangelo?

CAJETAN Oh yes. Well, in any case Raphael has now been made architect in charge—

LUTHER Who's Raphael?

CAJETAN *(sitting down)* I don't feel well. I think it's the climate.

LUTHER It is rather raw.

CAJETAN Yes. So, let's go back to the beginning. As I said at the outset, I wanted to offer you a word of sense.

LUTHER Very Reverend Father, I don't much hold with sense.

CAJETAN With what, then?

LUTHER Truth and faith.

CAJETAN What truth, what faith?

LUTHER The faith and the everlasting truth given us by God's word in this book. *(He has a Bible in his hand)*

CAJETAN The Bible?

LUTHER   The Holy Scriptures.

CAJETAN   Yes, yes, a fine book, I agree, particularly when you can't sleep. That is no doubt why it is always to be found lying around in inns.

LUTHER   It is God's word.

CAJETAN   Very possibly, but rather old by now, don't you find? Perhaps it's time we were writing new books.

LUTHER   God's word never grows old. It is everlasting and gives us everlasting certainty.

CAJETAN   There's a man, Copernicus, now who's published something. Extremely interesting. The earth turns about the sun and about itself. It's all much more complicated than we used to think.

LUTHER   We can gladly do without storybooks like that. Here is written everything we need to know about the earth.

CAJETAN   *(sitting down despondently)* The climate. It must be something in the climate. Well, supposing we have our official interview now. How do matters stand, do you recant?

LUTHER   I regret that I cannot recant.

CAJETAN   You have strict instructions?

LUTHER   Yes.

CAJETAN   From God or from the Elector?

LUTHER   Perhaps God has revealed himself to me through the Elector.

CAJETAN   Oh yes. (*He gives* LUTHER *a nod.* LUTHER *goes down from the platform. A* PRIEST *comes onto the platform*)

CAJETAN   We shall be hearing more of this. He still believes in God.

PRIEST   *(crossing himself, horror-struck)* Jesus Christ.

(All go off. End of the Diet)

TABLE LEFT FRONT

SPALATIN   Welcome to Wittenberg.

LUTHER   A fine welcome. I can hardly stand. Ten days on that old crock of a nag. Thank you.

SPALATIN   Horses' and monks' behinds are not really made for one another.

LUTHER   Your counselors were of a different opinion.

SPALATIN   Our people were a little too careful, although it was not necessary. But from below many things look differently.

LUTHER   I followed the counselors' instructions.

SPALATIN   Quite right. And perhaps, too, quite useful. A poor monk who on a sorry jade must flee through night and fog from the angry and powerful cardinal. A pretty picture. It gets talked about and lends something heroic to the affair.

LUTHER   *(feeling his behind)* You should all be beaten about the head with a Bible.

SPALATIN   News from Augsburg?

LUTHER   I did not recant.

SPALATIN   The Elector sends his thanks.

LUTHER   I composed with the counselors an appeal to the Pope. That's to say, I didn't really want to, but the counselors thought it would please the Prince.

SPALATIN   So it will.

LUTHER   I am relieved to hear it. One never knows what the Elector really wants.

SPALATIN   It's his manner.

LUTHER   If the Pope does not react—only a suggestion—we could appeal over the Pope's head to a General Council.

SPALATIN   Rather bold.

LUTHER   Not at all. The University of Paris also did that recently. I simply take the Sorbonne's text. The Pope can hardly find it amiss if I take my lead from the most Catholic of all universities.

SPALATIN   Clever. A thing like that will be very much to the Prince's taste. Strike first and play the innocent afterward.

LUTHER   I understand. And then—I thought—we could publish a document about the Augsburg discussions in which Cajetan is made to look a proper fool.

SPALATIN   Also good.

LUTHER   Which should I write first?

SPALATIN   Both. And have it printed at once, so that we have it on hand. For the document I can contribute something. *(He gives him a letter)* A letter from the Pope to Cajetan.

LUTHER   *(skimming it)* It says here that he can arrest me, and you told me there was no danger.

SPALATIN   The letter's out of date.

LUTHER   And in Augsburg?

SPALATIN   It was already out of date. Things keep moving all the time. Publish the letter in the document. It will give a good background for your flight. It makes the affair more dramatic and will attract notice.

LUTHER   But if the letter was out of date?

SPALATIN   Only we know that, don't we?

LUTHER   How, incidentally, have you got hold of a secret letter from the Pope to his Cardinal?

SPALATIN   I bribed his secretary.

LUTHER   Publish it all the same?

SPALATIN   All the same.

LUTHER   Friends advised me that the Prince should hide me in a safe place.

SPALATIN   Afraid?

LUTHER   I heard something about poison.

SPALATIN   Now you do exaggerate.

LUTHER   The idea doesn't come from me, you understand. People are concerned about me. More than I could be. I leave it to your cleverness to decide whether the advice is good.

SPALATIN   That's all been discussed. There's nothing for you and your friends to worry about.

LUTHER   And if there's trouble, the Elector can excuse himself as an ignorant layman who understands nothing of these matters and refer them to the University. And the University is on my side.

SPALATIN   You should have been a politician.

LUTHER   And if it comes to a trial—not in Rome. Only before German judges who are friendly with the Elector.

SPALATIN   As we agreed—although you wrote to Cajetan that you would submit yourself to the judgment of the Church.

LUTHER   *(embarrassed)* Yes, the things one writes.

SPALATIN   Yes.

LUTHER   But our agreements remain in force?

SPALATIN   Afraid after all?

LUTHER   Not for my own sake. I'm not concerned about myself. On the contrary. It pains me to be unworthy to suffer for the truth. I could have taken every calamity upon myself, but the

University. I am concerned about the University. Everybody knows it to be the darling of our Prince.

SPALATIN   Yes, that is known.

LUTHER   If I am removed the University will soon be closed.

SPALATIN   There are other professors.

LUTHER   Without me nobody will be able to maintain himself. And then what will become of these splendid students who are so wonderfully enthusiastic for the sciences? They'll flounder in ignorance. Where will they learn the truth? That worries me. I myself *(He stops himself with a nod)* I've exposed myself to enough trials and tribulations as it is.

SPALATIN   Tribulations? You had journey money and a pocketful of safe conducts. Was there anyone not compliant?

LUTHER   Oh no, everyone, very. As soon as I produced the Prince's letter of recommendation they were all very friendly and obliging. The people wondered at the safe conducts and kept referring to them. I was abundantly supplied with everything. Food and drink, all excellent. I've got really fat. If it hadn't been for that nag. Last time I was driven home in a carriage.

SPALATIN   We can't always be organizing triumphal processions. *(He is about to leave)*

LUTHER   And if it gets too much for the Prince I am quite willing to go to France.

SPALATIN   *(stopping in his tracks)* To France?

LUTHER   To the University of Paris.

SPALATIN   Just let that alone.

LUTHER   I should be glad to go.

SPALATIN   Monks should not be too clever. They have been known to fall off their high horses only because they despised an old nag.

LUTHER   *(bowing)* My humblest regards to the most gracious Prince Elector.

(SPALATIN *goes off.* LUTHER *goes right*)

TABLE LEFT FRONT

(MELANCHTHON *and* KARLSTADT *greet* LUTHER. MÜNZER *stands to one side.*)

KARLSTADT   Back alive?

LUTHER   I gave those worthies a piece of my mind. Cajetan, my goodness, is as much use at theology as a donkey at playing the harp. Yes, Brother Melanchthon, I wanted to sacrifice myself for you, for the young people and for the truth. We all have to die once. But God spurned me. I fear I am not worthy to suffer and be killed in such a cause. Such happiness will be granted to others, not to me. Who is this?

MELANCHTHON   Thomas Münzer.

LUTHER   Oh, so this is Münzer.

KARLSTADT   He wants to collaborate with us.

LUTHER   Then you're my man.

MÜNZER   I admire you, Doctor.

LUTHER   I'm sure you do. I have stormed Heaven and set the earth ablaze. No bishop and no theologian has ever dared to tackle such important matters.

KARLSTADT   I could name a few, my own theses among them.

LUTHER   Be that as it may. In Rome they're all at sixes and sevens and don't know what to do. I've heard they want to eliminate me by assassination and poison.

MELANCHTHON   Poison?

LUTHER   That's right.

MELANCHTHON   Perhaps the Prince should hide you for a while.

LUTHER   Tell that to Spalatin. I should have been destroyed long ago if Christ had not been leading me and my cause. My theses, my writings, everybody thought they would be the death of me. I myself on the journey to Augsburg saw nothing but the stake ahead of me. Well, I told the Lord God, if He wanted to have a game with me, He'd better take care or I'd be joining in. *(He gives a rumbling laugh)*

MÜNZER   The people are on your side. In all Germany.

LUTHER   That I know, that the people are on my side. And our lords and masters know it too.

MÜNZER   We must keep going now. On no account come to a standstill.

LUTHER   Have no fear. The cause will not be stifled. It comes from God. Unless of course my friends forsake me, as Christ was forsaken by his disciples. If the truth is left to stand alone, then it must preserve itself by its own hand. Not by mine.

KARLSTADT   Not by Spalatin's either?

LUTHER   Neither by mine nor by Spalatin's nor by that of any other man. And now I'm going to have a good mug of beer.

PLATFORM LEFT

FREDERICK   The Pope's sending a special legate. Cardinal Miltitz. The question is whether we should hide Luther or not.

FEILITZSCH   I was always against hiding him. The man's only useful while he goes on writing here. If we bury him somewhere the interest evaporates. We must on no account let him out of our hands. He must stay here; that's the only way he can help us with his writings.

FREDERICK   (to SPALATIN) You were for hiding him.

SPALATIN   I still am. But perhaps now we should postpone it till Miltitz has come and gone.

FREDERICK   So he stays here. We wait and see what Miltitz offers.

SPALATIN   We've already written to tell Luther that we'd rather have him elsewhere.

FREDERICK   Instructions revoked.

SPALATIN   He's already preaching farewell sermons.

FREDERICK   Then let him preach inaugural sermons.

SPALATIN   He's talking of France again.

FREDERICK   Still on that tack, is he? I say "somewhere else" and he hears "France." The lad's getting too clever.

FEILITZSCH   The King of France is determined to be German Emperor and has been sending wagonloads of ducats across the Rhine. Strange, hm?

FREDERICK   Has Luther been bribed?

SPALATIN   I don't think so. He's had a sniff of politics and is throwing his weight around.

FREDERICK   Let him worry about his theology. Politics is my affair. France, that would just suit him!

FEILITZSCH   Perhaps we ought to take him into our confidence a little. Otherwise, one of these days, for all our trouble, he'll go off in the wrong direction.

FREDERICK   Good. You do that, Spalatin. Go into retreat with him for a few days. Choose one of my castles. But don't tell him everything all at once.

SPALATIN   Of course not.

FREDERICK   So until Miltitz comes, it's truce. Let him compose a few more theological pieces. Something nice. Not a polemic. Something for the soul.

SPALATIN   But Your Electoral Grace, we already have—the things are already being delivered.

FREDERICK   What have we?

SPALATIN   The Augsburg Document.

FREDERICK   I told you you were responsible to me.

SPALATIN   I couldn't guess the Pope would be following up with a special legate. Besides which the papers have been lying for days in your in-basket. (*He takes a document from the table and hands it to* FREDERICK)

FREDERICK   Can't a man go hunting occasionally? (*He leafs through the document*) But this is now embarrassing.

SPALATIN   Recall it?

FREDERICK   That won't do either. Everyone'll think we've gone soft. (*He reads*) A forgery? But, children, that really won't do. First you steal from the Cardinal the Pope's secret letter. Then you publish it, and then on top of that you write that it's a forgery.

SPALATIN   Only because we thought—

FREDERICK   But, children, that's really going a bit too far. You mustn't go out of your way to cause offense. They're only human, like us. And we give them enough trouble as it is. That must come out without further ado.

SPALATIN   It's already printed.

FREDERICK   Then let the censorship black the passage over. (*He gives the document back to* SPALATIN) A forgery. Children, children, the things you come up with.

(*He goes off.* FEILITZSCH *and* SPALATIN *look at one another and shrug their shoulders*)

TABLE RIGHT FRONT

KARLSTADT   We must work together and take the next steps immediately.

MELANCHTHON   I think we ought first to analyze where we stand and what the next step should be.

KARLSTADT   That's what I thought.

LUTHER   Above all, Spalatin must be informed.

KARLSTADT   Always you and your court. Everyone knows what the court wants.

MELANCHTHON   I'm not so sure myself if we can entirely do without Spalatin.

KARLSTADT   I now have this disputation with Eck in Leipzig. It's going to be a tremendous thing. We've got a public forum there and I'll be letting them have it.

LUTHER   Good. I'll take that over.

KARLSTADT   You? How do you mean you?

LUTHER   I understand how to deal with the high-ups. Leave it to me.

KARLSTADT   But it was my theses that Eck attacked.

LUTHER   He also had theses of mine in mind.

MELANCHTHON   (to LUTHER) You can't do that to him. It's his book and his disputation. He's worked at it half a year. You can't just muscle in.

LUTHER   But it can all be traced back to me. Just leave it to me. (To KARLSTADT) I don't want you to be involved in such a trifling disputation. You've got much too good a head to waste it on such rubbish. I thought Eck would write about your important and serious work, instead of which he's making a great song and dance about my frivolities. But God knows that I can't do anything about it and that I must spend my life on these vain and silly trifles. (Pause. KARLSTADT and MELANCHTHON look at one another)

MÜNZER   These are unimportant questions. Should we not go direct to the peasants, working men and citizens? They'll join in. They're on our side, and it's their cause after all.

LUTHER   It's the cause of theology.

MÜNZER   I see it differently.

LUTHER   You haven't the inward vision.

MÜNZER   That may be. But what use is theology when outside there people are starving.

LUTHER   If they've lived Christian lives they'll go to Heaven.

MÜNZER It would be more Christian to give them something to eat.

LUTHER Tell that to the Prince.

MÜNZER Gladly. I'll take a few thousand half-starved, ragged peasants with me and see what he has to say to that.

LUTHER The peasant takes the ox's place without the horns over his face. *(He laughs)*

MÜNZER If the quarrel is only about who can give the best theological explanation for the fact that peasants are oxen, then it's not my quarrel.

LUTHER Nobody's asked you.

(MÜNZER, KARLSTADT, *and* MELANCHTHON *go off*)

PLATFORM LEFT

(FREDERICK *in an armchair, the* COURT FOOL *on his knees.* SPALATIN *comes onto the platform.*)

SPALATIN The Papal Chamberlain Miltitz.

MILTITZ *(dashing up the steps)* Your Supreme Electoral Grace—

FREDERICK This is my Court Fool. He can do the cardinals.

FOOL *(clutching his forehead, running up and down)* The climate, the climate, the climate, the climate.

MILTITZ Delicious.

FREDERICK He can do Maximilian too.

FOOL *(rummaging in his pockets)* I had a—just a moment, I did have a groat left. *(To* MILTITZ*)* Lend me a groat, lad. Just until later. We'll work out something. My word as Emperor. I'll pawn you my—I'll think of something—my glaciers. Just a groat.

MILTITZ Delicious.

FREDERICK Yes.

MILTITZ Your Supreme Electoral Highness. The Holy Father sends his son in Christ cordial greetings.

FREDERICK And what else?

MILTITZ A deed freeing your two illegitimate sons from the legal disabilities of illegitimate birth, so that they may without further ado be presented for the higher appointments and benefices of the Church.

FREDERICK   Accepted.

MILTITZ   I emphasize, *higher* appointments and benefices.

FREDERICK   Understood. I accept.

MILTITZ   Furthermore, new privileges for your famous collection of relics by which those who make the proper contribution will have their stay in purgatory shortened by a hundred years for every saint's bone in your collection.

FREDERICK   Accepted. (SPALATIN *calculates in a notebook*)

MILTITZ   Furthermore the Golden Rose of Virtue. The Holy Father writes—where did I put it then—ah, here. *(He reads aloud)* Beloved Son, the very holy Golden Rose was dedicated by us on the fourteenth day of the Holy Month of Lent, anointed with holy oil and sprinkled with fragrant incense under papal blessing. It is to be handed to you by our beloved son Charles von Miltitz —that's me—a man of noble blood and noble manners—that's me too. This Rose is the symbol of the most precious blood of Our Savior, by which we are saved. Therefore, dear son, let the divine fragrance penetrate the inmost heart of Your Highness, so that you may perform whatever the aforesaid Charles von Miltitz shall indicate to you. . . . Here's the pawn ticket. It's been deposited with Fugger. (FREDERICK *throws away the ticket in disappointment*) The highest decoration of Christendom.

FREDERICK   No doubt.

MILTITZ   Combined with new indulgences.

FREDERICK   Very good.

MILTITZ   Awarded for a pious mode of life.

FREDERICK   This will please my illegitimate sons.

MILTITZ   The Holy Father deplores the recent differences of opinion.

FREDERICK   So do I. So do I. But what can one do? Theology.

MILTITZ   You are so right. If I might exchange a few words with your professor. Perhaps one can mediate.

FREDERICK   Any time. Talk about anything you want to.

MILTITZ   I tender my most respectful thanks for Your Grace's audience. *(Goes off)*

FREDERICK   Pompous ass.

FOOL (*offering* FREDERICK *a withered flower*) A rotten stink-flower for the third illegitimate child.

FREDERICK Be off. (*To* SPALATIN) Have you worked it out?

SPALATIN For every bone a hundred more years. As we have a good variety of bones, with 18,970 relics the total of indulgences now comes to 1,902,202 years and 270 days.

FREDERICK 1,902,202 years. An increase of fifteen hundred per cent since we had Luther. You see, Spalatin, in big business one must make big investments. The affair is slowly beginning to pay off.

TABLE LEFT FRONT

(LUTHER *and* MILTITZ *sit with mugs of beer in front of them. Both have drunk a good deal. Laughter.*)

MILTITZ (*gives* LUTHER *a kiss on the left cheek, then goes around him and gives him a kiss on the right cheek*) And when I asked the people "What is the meaning of the Roman See to you?" they said "How should we know what kind of seat you have in Rome, whether wood or stone?" (*Both laugh, raising their mugs, toasting each other and drinking*)

LUTHER I'm glad you're here, Miltitz.

MILTITZ But you've given the Curia a few headaches, I can tell you, Doctor. Nothing like this has happened in a hundred years. They'd pay a million to dispose of the business once and for all. A million. A nice little sum.

LUTHER I was dragged into this quarrel by force. I only did it under compulsion. I suppose it was necessary. A concatenation of circumstances. But you can believe me, I didn't get involved of my own free will. It's not my fault. God is my witness.

MILTITZ The Pope has altered the rule about indulgences, my dear Doctor. It's now all according to your ideas. Just as you wanted it.

LUTHER Those accursed theses! I never wanted to distribute them. I wanted to dispute them at our University. With colleagues, then I'd have thrown them away after. But devil knows how, suddenly they keep cropping up all over the place. And yet I had deliberately phrased them in obscure and enigmatic language, and in such a form that I cannot conceive how the public understood them.

MILTITZ   I haven't understood them to this day.

LUTHER   There, you see, a lot of things weren't clear to me either. But all at once it's Luther here and Luther there. And what a sensation all these great people have made of the matter! I simply don't understand it. It's a wonder to me myself that these particular theses have caused such excitement. Others have written on the same subject. Nothing ever happened. I myself have published theses which were much sharper. Nothing happened. And it had to be this treatise which caught on. And yet—between ourselves—it really wasn't good.

MILTITZ   I think, though, some gentlemen found it very convenient.

LUTHER   I quickly sent it to my bishop and wrote that he should cross out what he wanted, so far as I was concerned he could throw the theses into the fire. I didn't attach any importance to them. But it was too late. I even wanted to write a book about the power of the indulgence so as to obliterate these theses which were being distributed against my will. *(He shrugs his shoulders and drinks)*

MILTITZ   There are many who say the Prince is behind it all.

LUTHER   If you hadn't contradicted them, everything would long have been forgotten. The song would have vanished from everybody's lips.

MILTITZ   You ask rather a lot of the Pope. The Holy Father was really patient.

LUTHER   But now there must be an end. If an end isn't made now and the quarrel goes on, then the affair really will become public property and instead of theological theses we shall have deadly earnest. Therefore it's best for us now to keep quiet. You'll be silent and I'll be silent. Then the affair will bleed to death.

MILTITZ   Yes, I agree. *(He drinks)*

LUTHER   You'll instruct the Archbishop of Treves—he's a good friend of the Prince—to name the articles in which I have erred, then I'll be glad to recant.

MILTITZ   No difficulty about that. As I told you, the Pope has changed the indulgence. But perhaps one should also issue a proclamation to the people, that they should be loyal and obedient to the Church.

LUTHER   Good idea. I'll do that. A proclamation to the people. Loyal and obedient. That's good.

MILTITZ   There's a deal of unrest about. Everywhere they're against the Church and the authorities. Absolutely horrifying. Three out of four of those I asked were for you.

LUTHER   Do you think I should make another apology to the Pope?

MILTITZ   Not a bad idea. Our masters love that.

LUTHER   Certainly I was too heated. But I wrote to the Pope at the time that I threw myself at his feet with everything that I was and had. He was to approve or disapprove, pronounce life or death. I submit myself. Instead of that he hounds me with diplomats.

MILTITZ   These chanceries . . . you know what they are. The Pope wants peace and quiet.

LUTHER   So do I. I am ready to do and suffer anything, only to make an end of the affair. I want in all humility to honor the Church. I will gladly recant and be silent for evermore.

MILTITZ   Beloved brother. *(He throws his arms about his neck and kisses him)*

NEWSPAPER BOY   *(selling a special edition)* Emperor Maximilian dead. Emperor Maximilian dead. *(People rush to buy the papers)*

PLATFORM RIGHT

(Three gentlemen seated on chairs. SCHWARZ stands writing at the high desk. FUGGER ascends the platform.)

SCHWARZ   Special partners' meeting of the firm of Jacob Fugger. Sole item on the agenda: Providing a new German Emperor.

FUGGER   *(crossing himself)* Praised be Jesus Christ.

ALL   For ever and ever, Amen.

FUGGER   Gentlemen, I see three candidates. The King of France, Frederick of Saxony, and Charles. You have the statement of our production and development section. For our purposes Charles is probably the most suitable. He is young, we can make long-term arrangements with him. He secures us our existing possessions, mines, metallurgical plant, et cetera. He brings us the Netherlands, the most important center of commerce for the coming centuries. He brings us Spain and with it the mercury mines.

He brings us America, whose gold and silver deliveries are becoming more and more important. He offers us the possibility of a major entry into the spice trade. He will have to wage wars. Since we have turned a great part of our plant over to armament production, we need a new large-scale customer. From Maximilian he has inherited the weakness for artillery and our cannons are a quality article. Besides, as you know, every shot uses a hundredweight of copper and copper we know is bought from us. A further consideration is that his chief enemy will be the Pope, and since the Pope is also our customer our profits will double. No other candidate offers us such possibilities of profit.

1ST GENTLEMAN   The King of France has already paid a great deal. Most of the electors have taken his money. So they will vote for him.

FUGGER   I have let the gentlemen concerned know that I will pay double what the King of France pays.

2ND GENTLEMAN   And the Saxon? He has good prospects.

FUGGER   From the point of view of internal politics he is undoubtedly the stronger, but he doesn't bring us the international business.

1ST GENTLEMAN   But he can cause trouble.

FUGGER   Yes.

2ND GENTLEMAN   Can he just be passed over like that?

3RD GENTLEMAN   I warn you. He's a sly old fox, that one. He can think around corners.

1ST GENTLEMAN   And he's the only one left who knows his way about Empire politics.

FUGGER   An outstanding politician, without a doubt. If you ask me, the only one we have. But I think I have made his limits clear to him.

3RD GENTLEMAN   Charles can be expensive.

FUGGER   It's the hour of the princes. They must have princely payment.

1ST GENTLEMAN   How much?

FUGGER   I'm reckoning on a hundred million. We shall form a syndicate. But I'm absolutely determined. We'll do this business. Any objections? (*The* THREE GENTLEMEN *shake their heads*) Then Charles will be German Emperor. I declare the meeting closed. (*He crosses himself*) Praise be to Jesus Christ. (FUGGER *and the* THREE GENTLEMEN *go off*)

SCHWARZ *(slowly recording)* For ever and ever, Amen. Full stop.
(He goes off)

TABLE RIGHT FRONT

BIBBIENA If Charles gets in, we can shut up shop here. *(To the* POPE) He'll turn you into his court chaplain.

2ND CARDINAL Shouldn't we have another word with France?

POPE *(shaking his head)* That's out. Fugger has more money.

2ND CARDINAL Why don't we withdraw the contracts from Fugger?

POPE Because Fugger will then withdraw his money from us. If anyone can still save us it's the Saxon. You know him, Cajetan. How can one get at him?

CAJETAN One can't ever get at him.

BIBBIENA He'll take money, surely?

CAJETAN If he can't get anything better.

BIBBIENA Anyone who can't be bribed lacks character in other respects too.

CAJETAN He doesn't lack character. But he's such a difficult customer. He's always telling everyone that he takes no bribes.

POPE So what does he want?

CAJETAN Ask me what Charles wants, what Henry VIII wants, what Francis I wants, what the Sultan wants, but don't ask me what that Frederick wants. Every time you think you've concluded an agreement with him you find him with his foot in the door again.

POPE The Luther affair. I know. He diddled you there.

CAJETAN He'll diddle Miltitz too. He operates through Luther.

POPE You can never get at Frederick himself. Let's write a letter to Luther. *(To the* 2ND CARDINAL, *who takes notes)* Ask him to Rome. I'll be a gentle father to him. The Lord saith, "I rejoice not in the death of a sinner, but that he should repent and live." And arrange for generous traveling expenses. *(To the others)* Don't let anyone attack Luther. Let him write what he wants. He must be packed in cotton wool.

BIBBIENA And what do you want to do with him?

POPE Some castle somewhere. An estate in the Campagna. Something like that. Once he sees the sun he'll begin writing differently.

BIBBIENA   Love poems?

POPE   Perhaps.

CAJETAN   If you think you can buy this man off the Saxon, you're asking for a miracle.

POPE   The Church lives on miracles as others on bread.

BIBBIENA   And the miracle Charles?

POPE   Now don't ask me to start praying as well. Why can't this Frederick be Emperor?

CAJETAN   If he wants, he will be.

POPE   Has he prospects?

CAJETAN   Better than Charles. He orders the German princes about as he pleases.

POPE   Then let him be Emperor. (*To the* 2ND CARDINAL) An express messenger to Miltitz. He is to visit Frederick. Write to the Prince that I am entirely on his side and that I'll do everything I can for him. I will recognize him as Emperor even if he can only collect two votes. (*To* CAJETAN) Can he?

CAJETAN   Easily.

POPE   So, two votes, and I'll make him Emperor.

BIBBIENA   Luther?

POPE   Write that he may appoint Luther a cardinal and present him with a large—no, a very large—archbishopric.

TABLE LEFT FRONT

(*The* COURT FOOL *is standing on the table in the robes of a cardinal.*)

FREDERICK   (*laughing*) What is that?

FOOL   Luther as cardinal. (*He takes off the robe and puts on a crown*)

FREDERICK   And that?

FOOL   Frederick of Saxony as German Emperor.

FREDERICK   (*laughing*) Not bad. German Emperor. Two votes. It could be done. What do you think, Spalatin?

SPALATIN   If I may speak openly?

FREDERICK   That's what I pay you for.

SPALATIN   Your Electoral Grace should carefully consider the matter.

FREDERICK   Then you consider it.

SPALATIN   The Pope, thanks to Luther, we have more or less eliminated. What he could offer us, we already have. Perhaps an indulgence here, a blessing there. That'll butter no parsnips.

FREDERICK   Correct.

SPALATIN   Fugger offers seven million and Charles' sister for your nephew. So, what have we to expect from the Pope: nothing. What have we to expect from Fugger: a great deal. What happens if we take sides against the Pope: nothing. What happens if we take sides against Fugger: a great deal.

FREDERICK   Right again. What can Fugger do?

SPALATIN   What can't he do? If we spoil the election for him, he'll do us in. Perhaps we'll be able to hold out two years, but he'll ruin us.

FREDERICK   Wrong. We sha'n't hold out even a year. But what's to be done with Charles? When a young lad like that comes to the throne, he's apt to think the whole world belongs to him.

SPALATIN   That may be an advantage. Charles is ruler over so many lands. Everywhere insurrections, trouble with the nobility, wars with France, with the Pope. When'll he be able to bother about Germany? He'll pay us a few visits, that's all. And when he's away, Your Electoral Grace is Vice-Regent of the Empire. So what will be changed? Nothing.

FREDERICK   Right again. But if that doesn't satisfy me?

SPALATIN   Force through a severe electoral treaty, limiting his rights.

FREDERICK   And if the treaty's so severe that he practically cannot rule at all?

SPALATIN   Your voice is the most important. They'll sign anything for you.

FREDERICK   But an emperor who can't rule, what sort of thing is that?

SPALATIN   *(considering)* An imperial government will have to be set up—ah, I understand.

FREDERICK   I'm glad you do. A small body of illustrious gentlemen to rule Germany.

SPALATIN   And since you are in any case the chief man in this body, you rule Germany. You'll lack only the title. But in return you get seven million and the Emperor's sister in your family. That's good business.

FREDERICK   I'm glad to see that in my service you've learned to think. *(He pulls a document out of his pocket)* Here's the electoral treaty.

SPALATIN   *(taking the treaty)* You will be called Frederick the Wise.

FREDERICK   So I should hope.

PLATFORM LEFT

(CHARLES V *and* MARGARET *on a couch. She is reading a book to him.*)

MARGARET   Machiavelli, *The Prince*, Chapter 18: "How Far Rulers Should Keep Their Word." Experience teaches that, in our times especially, those rulers do best who take little account of good faith and are skilled dissemblers and deceivers of men. And in the end they have gained the upper hand of those who based themselves on honesty. You must know that there are two kinds of weapon: right and might. Thus a ruler must be a fox and a lion. A clever ruler can and may break his word if it would injure him to keep it. But rulers have never lacked righteous reasons for giving color to a breach of faith. We could cite innumerable examples from recent times to show how many peace treaties and promises have not been kept. The one who has best understood how to play the fox has come off best. All that is required is to put a good exterior on the fox's nature and to be a master of hypocrisy and disguise. It is therefore not necessary that a ruler should possess virtues provided he seems to possess them. Thus a ruler must make a display of gentleness, loyalty, humanity, honesty, and piety but when necessary turn them into their opposites. Especially the fear of God is indispensable for him. For men judge in general by their eyes. Everybody sees what the ruler seems to be. Only few understand how he really is, and these few do not dare to stand against the opinion of the multitude, which moreover has the majesty of the State on its side.

(GATTINARA *comes onto the platform*)

GATTINARA   Your Majesty, Fugger will pay, and Frederick has agreed. So you are now master of Europe and the rest of the world.

MARGARET   But for a few small territories.

CHARLES   Which I shall conquer. In the way I have learned from you, Aunt. (*He pries at one of her thighs*) Lower Italy I have already. (*He pries at the other thigh*) Then I take Upper Italy. (*He clasps her between the legs*) And then I go clap. And the Pope is in my hand.

MARGARET   But Your Majesty, isn't that very dangerous?

CHARLES   Not for me. For the Pope.

MARGARET   And Switzerland?

CHARLES   Where's that?

MARGARET   Further up.

CHARLES   (*clasping her breast*) Here?

MARGARET   Your Majesty.

CHARLES   Mountains. We'll have losses.

MARGARET   And France?

CHARLES   I'll crucify France. (*He presses* MARGARET *back. She lies stretched before him*) Anything else missing?

MARGARET   The attack.

GATTINARA   Aha.

CHARLES   (*turning around*) Politics, Gattinara. We must face realities. (*He sits down again*)

GATTINARA   I see Madame has a knockdown method.

MARGARET   (*getting up again*) The Emperor must be initiated while still young.

CHARLES   My Aunt has always helped me in outstanding matters.

GATTINARA   In outstanding matters Madame has abundant experience.

MARGARET   Which must be passed on to the young people.

GATTINARA   Undoubtedly.

CHARLES   Do you suppose I could know otherwise where Switzerland is?

GATTINARA   Or how the Pope is to be caught.

MARGARET   Or how France is to be conquered.

GATTINARA   Oh, he knows that too now, does he? Your Majesty, I see there is no further hindrance to your rule.

PLATFORM RIGHT

(*In front of the platform* FREDERICK, ALBERT, *and five other* ELECTORS *are standing.* FUGGER *and* SCHWARZ *on the platform.*)

SCHWARZ   (*striking a balance*) The most expensive Emperor we've ever had.

FUGGER   How much?

SCHWARZ   85,191,800. That's only what passes through the books.

FUGGER   Then I have correctly evaluated our gentlemen.

SCHWARZ   A major investment.

FUGGER   Remind me that I'm founding a chapel. In big business one should always make God a shareholder. For safety's sake.

SCHWARZ   Where shall I enter it? Under mortgages or new issues?

FUGGER   Board of management.

SCHWARZ   Time to pay out? (FUGGER *nods.* SCHWARZ *calls out*) Bribes forward! (*The* ELECTORS *do not stir*)

FUGGER   *Douceurs!*

SCHWARZ   I'll never learn. (*He calls out*) Douceurs forward!

(*The* ELECTORS *hurriedly advance onto the platform.* SCHWARZ *at his desk. They range themselves before him,* ALBERT *first*)

SCHWARZ   (*giving him a check*) Your check.

ALBERT   And a fourth bishopric. (FUGGER *nods*) And cardinal legate. (FUGGER *nods.* ALBERT *gives* SCHWARZ *his ballot*) For Charles.

1ST ELECTOR   (SCHWARZ *gives him the check*) A moment. (*He scrutinizes the check*) Correct. (*He hands over his ballot*) Charles.

2ND ELECTOR   Two million more.

FUGGER   No.

2ND ELECTOR   Then it'll become a matter of conscience.

FUGGER   We've bought Sickingen. He's stationed in front of the town. His force is in good fighting trim.

2ND ELECTOR   I have troops too. (*He steps out of line*)

3RD ELECTOR   (SCHWARZ *gives him his check; he gives* SCHWARZ *his ballot*) For Charles.

4TH ELECTOR (*likewise*) For Charles.

5TH ELECTOR (*likewise*) For Charles.

2ND ELECTOR (*coming forward again*) I have consulted my conscience. One million.

FUGGER (*pointing to the ballots*) The majority's here already. I could even deduct something from you.

2ND ELECTOR (*taking the check and tossing over the ballot*) For Charles. (FREDERICK *steps forward*)

SCHWARZ Your check.

FREDERICK (*taking the check*) This is of course only the repayment of an old debt.

FUGGER What debt is that?

FREDERICK An old debt. It looks better in the books.

FUGGER But of course. All part of the service.

FREDERICK And is governed by the banker's seal of secrecy.

FUGGER As always. (FREDERICK *is about to go*) Prince! Your Ballot.

FREDERICK My apologies. (*He gives* SCHWARZ *the ballot*) For Charles. Out of conviction.

FUGGER The gentlemen may proceed to the electoral chapel.

PLATFORM LEFT

(*On the platform a small table and a few stools. The* ELECTORS *march ceremonially onto the platform. In front of the platform two trumpeters. On the platform, his face to the audience, a* MASTER OF CEREMONIES. *The public gathers. A bell tolls.*)

MASTER OF CEREMONIES Let no one be afraid. This is ancient custom. When the storm bell tolls, let everyone fall to his knees and pray to God with all his heart to grant the Electors grace to choose an emperor advantageous to God Almighty, to the Holy Empire and to all of us. (*The crowd kneels and prays*) The Electors will be seated.

(FREDERICK *and two other* ELECTORS *sit down.* FREDERICK *pulls out a pack of cards, shuffles them and deals. The other* ELECTORS *stand round looking bored*)

MASTER OF CEREMONIES   The Electors will give their votes.
FREDERICK   18, 20, and the 1, 3, 4, 7, 30. (*The other* ELECTORS *pass.* FREDERICK *picks up the cards*) A Christian game. Clubs solo, gentlemen. (*He leads*)
ALBERT   Smells so stuffy here. Don't you smell it? Stuffy.
FREDERICK   Quiet!
2ND ELECTOR   (*looking over the shoulder of one of the card-playing* ELECTORS) The King. The King. Why man, he's playing clubs.
FREDERICK   Well, gentlemen, are we playing or not?
MASTER OF CEREMONIES   Frederick of Saxony has doubts.
4TH ELECTOR   Shall we go drinking after?
5TH ELECTOR   What else?
ALBERT   Do you know this one? A bishop comes naked out of the confessional —
FREDERICK   Clubs, clubs, clubs. (*He slams each card down on the table*)
MASTER OF CEREMONIES   The Electors are counting the votes. Pray to God. Pray.
FREDERICK   (*adding up his tricks*) 24, 30, 38, 45, 50, 68. That does it, gentlemen, clubs with one. A cheap game.
MASTER OF CEREMONIES   (*shouting*) It is Charles.

(*Fanfares, peals of bells, organ music. The* ELECTORS *march down from the platform. The crowd cheers them*)

PLATFORM RIGHT

(CHARLES *lies with his legs on an armchair and his head in his aunt's la, .*)
GATTINARA   (*coming onto the platform*) Charles V, by God's Grace Roman Emperor-elect, King of the Romans, ever Augustus, King of Spain, Germany, Sicily, Jerusalem, Hungary, Dalmatia, Croatia, the Balearics, the Canary and Indian Isles and the Continent beyond the Ocean, Archduke of Austria, Duke of Burgundy, Brabant, Styria, Carinthia, Carniola, Luxemburg, Limburg, Athens, and Neopatria, Count of Hapsburg, Flanders, Tirol, Count-Palatinate of Burgundy, Hennegau, Pfirt, Roussil-

lon, Landgrave in Alsace, Prince in Swabia, Lord in Asia and Africa.

CHARLES *(has been counting them up on his fingers)* Correct, Charles V tra-la-la, tra-la-la, tra-la-la. Nice, isn't it, Aunt?

MARGARET Very nice, my treasure.

CHARLES Is there anyone who has a longer title?

GATTINARA I don't know of any, Your Majesty.

CHARLES Lucky for him. I should have had to cut his head off.

GATTINARA Your Majesty. Since it has pleased God in His unique grace to raise you above all the kings and princes of Christendom to a power previously possessed only by Charles the Great, you are now on the way to world dominion.

CHARLES In the service of God.

GATTINARA Didn't I say so.

CHARLES I didn't hear it.

GATTINARA In the service of God, to the gathering of Christendom under one lord.

CHARLES Lord?

GATTINARA Ah, shepherd of course. Gathering under one shepherd. The program of government. The fear of God and humility.

CHARLES Evidently.

GATTINARA A sovereign deportment. If you can't think of anything, be silent. Everyone will suppose you have clever thoughts.

CHARLES Charles the Silent.

GATTINARA Observance of wills and treaties, but only when advantageous.

CHARLES Charles the Executor.

GATTINARA Sensible laws, order in your finances.

CHARLES Charles the Debtor.

GATTINARA As a coat of arms of course there is no question of anything but the two-headed eagle with heart-point and quarterings. The seal to vary from one territory to another. For all important and secret matters the Seal of Majesty, the Emperor enthroned with orb and scepter, the imperial arms dexter, the royal arms sinister, for Burgundy with St. Andrew's Cross or the Pillars of Hercules.

MARGARET Make it the Pillars, darling.

GATTINARA With that a small privy council.

CHARLES   That will be you two and Erasmus.

GATTINARA   Erasmus?

CHARLES   He has beautiful thoughts.

MARGARET   Erasmus won't come.

CHARLES   Money.

GATTINARA   Money all the time, but he'll never come.

CHARLES   But I will it.

GATTINARA   But he does not will it.

CHARLES   Filthy trickster.

GATTINARA   If I may summarize therefore, be open-handed, dishonest, mendacious, faithless and—moderate yourself somewhat.

CHARLES   What in?

GATTINARA   Auntie will explain that to you. And for the business
of the day. Deal with the most important things every morning
the moment you get up, if not while you're still dressing.

CHARLES   Auntie always helps me with that in any case.

MARGARET   Don't overburden the child. I find him weak enough
as it is.

GATTINARA   Exactly. Perhaps Madame will have the humanity
to remember.

MARGARET   Remember what?

GATTINARA   Madame has already lost two husbands by enfeeble-
ment.

MARGARET   They didn't complain.

GATTINARA   But if you could perhaps be sparing of the German
Emperor. The title has cost too much money as it is.

MARGARET   Why is it always the women who have to give up
things.

GATTINARA   Charles would no doubt put a guard regiment at your
disposal.

MARGARET   Would you do that, treasure?

CHARLES   I'll consider it.

GATTINARA   At field strength, if I may advise.

(CHARLES, MARGARET, *and* GATTINARA *go down off the
platform. They meet* FREDERICK *and the other* ELECTORS
in the middle of the stage)

CHARLES   Uncle.

FREDERICK   My dear boy. *(They embrace)* I am so proud.

CHARLES   I no German. You speak French?

FREDERICK   No.

CHARLES   Speak Spanish?

FREDERICK   Nay, Saxon.

CHARLES   I rule only with Uncle.

FREDERICK   A good boy. A dear boy. *(In a lower voice)* When is the wedding?

CHARLES   Wedding?

FREDERICK   Your sister is promised to my nephew.

CHARLES   Not understand.

FREDERICK   Wedding, sister, nephew.

CHARLES   I today celebration.

FREDERICK   I'll ram your celebration down your—

CHARLES   *(seizing* FREDERICK's *hand)* Thanks for congratulations.

FREDERICK   The electoral treaty. *(An* ELECTOR *gives him the document)* All freedoms and privileges of the princes are preserved. The princes form an imperial government. Without our consent no war, no alliance, no treaty, no Diet, no taxes. No foreign troops in Germany. Whatever is won in a war belongs to us. All offices are to be occupied by Germans. Diets to be held only in Germany. And—no German to be brought before a court of law outside the Empire. Moreover, nobody to be put under the imperial ban without a hearing, but he gets a proper trial. Is that clear?

GATTINARA   Is that the Luther clause?

FREDERICK   Who Luther? Not understand.

CHARLES   Spain fine.

FREDERICK   You oath. Treaty. (CHARLES *raises his hand for the oath)* Speak after me—*(Low)* What about the wedding?

CHARLES   Not understand.

FREDERICK   You—promise.

CHARLES   Go to hell—

FREDERICK   *(aloud)* So help me God.

CHARLES   So help me God.

GATTINARA   Haven't you got handcuffs for him as well?

FREDERICK   *(pointing to the treaty)* This is enough.

MARGARET   Can you tell me how the boy is now to rule?

FREDERICK   Am I the Emperor?

(GATTINARA *and* MARGARET *with the other* PRINCES *go behind*)

FREDERICK   *(taking* CHARLES *aside)* Tell me, the Princes have commissioned me to ask, how about women?
CHARLES   Women?
FREDERICK   Yes. Well, my colleagues think, there are these rumors, you're still young, you understand?
CHARLES   Women beautiful.
FREDERICK   Certainly. I only think . . . well, women think . . . that's to say—after all it's important.
CHARLES   Women?
FREDERICK   Isn't there a cardinal here? Well here, goddammit, you with women—*(He strikes one hand in another)* Like that.
CHARLES   Ah. Fuck.
FREDERICK   That's it.
CHARLES   *(turns round and calls)* Auntie! *(He goes off behind)*
FREDERICK   Strange boy.

PLATFORM LEFT

(FREDERICK *walks onto the platform.* SPALATIN *awaits him*)

FREDERICK   What is it?
SPALATIN   Luther. *(gives him a letter)*
FREDERICK   What kind of muck-up has he been making this time?
SPALATIN   He's started a quarrel with the Bishop of Meissen.
FREDERICK   God in Heaven! What do I pay the man for? To get embroiled with any old bishops or professors? Has he gone mad? It'll only cause trouble and bring no return. The Bishop is paid by the other side, so he has a different opinion. Once and for all, this messing around with trivialities has got to stop. Luther will write to the bishops and apologize. I will see the letter. I want everything he writes to be checked and corrected. He is to deliver his letters and manuscripts here. I am fed up with it, once and for all.
SPALATIN   Then there's the letter from the Pope to Luther.

FREDERICK   The peace overture?

SPALATIN   Including travel expenses.

FREDERICK   Lose it.

SPALATIN   If Luther hears about the letter?

FREDERICK   No letter has been received here. That's the last straw. If he reads three friendly words from the Pope, he'll immediately offer himself for crucifixion. The business with Miltitz was quite enough. Here am I thinking I'd bought a fighter of God and it turns out that the gentleman would much prefer to hide. It shows a downright lack of character. And now, of all things. Have you heard the news? Hutten, Sickingen, the Knights. The gentlemen are setting up their own party. The gentlemen are turning "national." A unified German Empire under a strong Emperor Charles, and the Princes to the gallows.

SPALATIN   It's only a bid for the property of the Church.

FREDERICK   Of course. What else? The gentlemen want to make themselves solvent. They're indebted up to the hilt. Only the Church estates can save them.

SPALATIN   My information is that they want Your Electoral Grace to join them.

FREDERICK   Because I've got Luther.

SPALATIN   They hope for your support.

FREDERICK   Thanks, I'll drive my own bargain. Fugger was right. The boom in indulgences is over, the market's changing. If that happens, we'd do best to turn the whole Church into cash. Do you know that two-thirds of German landed estate belong to the Church? Two-thirds! Have you ever calculated how many monasteries, endowments, and churches there are in my country? And all are full of treasures and works of art, collected for centuries. Precious tapestries. Gold and silver utensils. A deal involving thousands of millions. The deal of the century. I dream of it at night. But I need a reason. A hard-and-fast reason. Statements of claim I have in plenty. Mountains high. The acts of the Diet. Reports for Maximilian. Books of Hutten. All petitions; I need solid reasons. I cannot simply pocket the wealth of the Church. There must be an explanation. Hutten says "national." I'm a Christian prince. I can only expropriate if by that I perform a task pleasing to God.

SPALATIN   I'll set the whole team to work. Melanchthon is a crafty lad.

FREDERICK   All in Luther's name. The man has been introduced and a good brand name should not be changed. Besides, I love it when he opens his mouth; he talks like a cabbie. It immediately suggests a holy wrath holding the world up to ridicule.

SPALATIN   Only our young people haven't the right insight into the business side.

FREDERICK   Give them the documentation. And put at their disposal a man who knows. The gentlemen must interpret God's word in such a way that I can do something with it and that the people understand.

SPALATIN   The people understand "nationally."

FREDERICK   Whoever says national means money.

SPALATIN   Whoever says Christian means money.

FREDERICK   Let's say Christian–National, then we'll collect twice over.

TABLE LEFT FRONT

LUTHER   Has the Pope written?

SPALATIN   No.

LUTHER   Will he impose the ban?

SPALATIN   We must expect it.

LUTHER   I have always declared myself ready for anything. Why am I condemned? I have promised so often to obey the Church. I am ready at any time to modify my views. The Church must decide, I will conform. I wrote to the Pope that I'd do anything he wanted. Why doesn't he answer?

SPALATIN   Heaven knows.

LUTHER   But he could at least give me a hearing. He can't simply outlaw me.

SPALATIN   That's the sort of people they are.

LUTHER   I am a Professor of Theology. It is my duty to dispute theses. It's what all professors do. Why am I something special?

SPALATIN   You've written a great deal.

LUTHER   My books. Their circulation gives me nothing but trouble. My dearest wish is that they should all vanish.

SPALATIN   That's no longer possible. You've now become "that
Luther."

LUTHER   I want nothing any more but to be released from my pro-
fessorship and bury myself in some corner. I occupy this chair
against my will. It causes me nothing but trouble. Speak to the
Prince. Ask him to dismiss me.

SPALATIN   The Prince would throw me out if I came to him with
such a suggestion. Besides, he has a nice new job for you. Something political. Not theology.

LUTHER   You play your politics and I go to the stake for it afterward.

SPALATIN   Put your entire trust in the Prince.

LUTHER   And if the Prince changes his mind?

SPALATIN   I have faith that he won't.

LUTHER   A fine faith. Pray God that He may preserve it for us.

SPALATIN   You have always been well looked after till now.

LUTHER   Till now.

SPALATIN   What do you want? to go to other princes? Their minds
too may change. Back into the lap of the Church? Their mind it's
true does not change.

LUTHER   That bastard of a Pope, lousy stinker, syphlitic bitch,
crazy, hellish, lying shit.

SPALATIN   That's the right tone.

TABLE RIGHT FRONT

HUTTEN   (calling) Luther!
LUTHER   Hutten. (They embrace)
HUTTEN   You hero of the nation. Still managing to avoid the stake?
LUTHER   The Prince protects me.
HUTTEN   I wouldn't be so sure of that.
LUTHER   How so?
HUTTEN   Oh, we hear things.
LUTHER   What things?
HUTTEN   Extradition.
LUTHER   Who says that?
HUTTEN   Rumors. Nothing precise. Only, don't put too much trust
in princes. They're fickle gentry.

LUTHER   In whom should I put my trust?

HUTTEN   Join us, the Knights' Party. Sickingen will protect you. He offers you asylum in his castle.

LUTHER   That *is* a piece of news.

HUTTEN   I have more like it. Here's a letter from Schaumburger. He puts a hundred knights at your disposal. For your protection.

LUTHER   *(taking the letter)* A hundred knights, *(Laughing)* one hundred knights.

HUTTEN   And behind them stands Sickingen with his army.

LUTHER   And I can go to his castle any time?

HUTTEN   Any time. Join us. My motto is "The die is cast. I have dared it."

LUTHER   Then for me too the die is cast. I despise the children of Rome, whether in wrath or favor. Forever I reject all reconciliation, all community with them. Let the children of Rome come. Let them threaten. Let them flatter. I will have nothing more to do with them.

HUTTEN   What do you think of a proclamation? You are famous. You are revered. The people listen to you.

LUTHER   That fits in well. I've got to write a leaflet for the nobility as it is.

HUTTEN   You can freely trust me with all your plans.

LUTHER   It's high time. We must make a clean sweep at last. I'll write a proclamation which will bring the people running.

HUTTEN   And write above all what the people would like to hear. And write that they should venture something themselves. The Church must go. And the princes of the Church. You must thoroughly stir them up.

LUTHER   It must not depend on that.

HUTTEN   We must also elicit the Elector's attitude. If he will join us, if he wants to stay neutral, or if in an emergency we can retreat into his territory. If he will cooperate, our cause is won.

LUTHER   And if not?

HUTTEN   Have no fear. The whole nobility is behind us, and you will bring the people. We have arms and fists enough for our enterprise. All you have to do is to write. Write a great deal. It will be worth it, believe me.

LUTHER   I can go to Sickingen's castle any time?

HUTTEN   Put your entire trust in Sickingen. *(He points to the letter)* Here are one hundred men ready and waiting for you.

LUTHER   For the Knights' Party.

HUTTEN   For freedom, fatherland, and Church estates.

LUTHER   You must not think the cause of the gospel can be furthered without noise, trouble, and insurrection. You cannot make swans-down out of a sword. And you can't make peace out of war. The word of God is trouble, ruin and poison, sword, war and revolution.

HUTTEN   That's the right tone.

TABLE LEFT FRONT

LUTHER   *(giving* SPALATIN *a packet of letters)* Here are over thirty letters of thanks from princes and other eminent gentlemen thanking me for the epistolary pamphlet *To the Christian Nobility of the German Nation.* The eminent gentlemen are very pleased with me.

SPALATIN   So are we, my dear Doctor, so are we. The Prince is just writing to the Pope again in your cause.

LUTHER   What is he writing?

SPALATIN   He's still playing the innocent. He will insist that your errors are proved to you.

LUTHER   Excellent. Perhaps the Prince could also mention that my views are very widespread in Germany, and that the Pope will achieve nothing at all by violence and outlawry. He can write that he considers it his duty to warn the Pope. That the Germans are an obstinate people and that it would be dangerous to provoke them.

SPALATIN   That is a declaration of war.

LUTHER   It will make an impression on those cowardly dogs. Perhaps you would also show the Prince this document. A letter from a friend who will protect me with a hundred knights.

SPALATIN   Interesting.

LUTHER   I should much like the Prince also to tell the Pope about it in writing. He should be made aware that the imperial ban will only make things worse. There are in Germany men who can and will protect me. And under the protection of the knights I shall

attack much more vigorously than under the supervision of the
Prince. I no longer need to take any notice of the Prince.

SPALATIN   Who are you trying to impress? The Pope or the Prince?

LUTHER   I only wanted to make it known. Use it as you will. Incidentally, some people think the Prince should get me an edict
from the Emperor, to forbid me being proscribed.

SPALATIN   Are you negotiating about this with other parties?

LUTHER   I? I know nothing about that. Why?

SPALATIN   Sickingen's castle is very drafty. I can't recommend it
to you. And the Swiss scheme I should also refuse if I were you,
even though a lot of money is offered.

LUTHER   People want to help me.

SPALATIN   All the same I should advise you not to leave Wittenberg.

LUTHER   Am I the Prince's prisoner?

SPALATIN   The Prince protects his subjects on all sides. Moreover
I recommend you to study the artillery textbook, chapter 4:
"Destruction of Knights' Castles."

LUTHER   My dear Spalatin, I have built my cause on God.

SPALATIN   I am glad of it for your sake.

LUTHER   *(bowing)* My most humble respects to His Electoral Grace.

(SPALATIN *goes off*)

PLATFORM LEFT

(FREDERICK *has his* FOOL *on his lap*)

FOOL   *(in a piping voice)* Jesus loves me, this I know. For the Bible
tells me so. (SPALATIN *comes onto the platform with books*)

FREDERICK   Such a sweet little voice. I could hug him. (*To* SPALA-
TIN) Have I got to read all that?

SPALATIN   If Your Electoral Grace will bring professors into the
world, Your Electoral Grace will harvest books. That is their
revenge.

FREDERICK   But, my children, you can't do this to me. (SPALATIN
presses a book into his hand) No, no, I won't. Come, you're all
my dear children, let's play Tarot or sing a song. (SPALATIN
opens a book) I don't understand all this. *To the Christian Nobility of the German Nation.*

SPALATIN   Your Electoral Grace has hatched out Luther; now Your
Electoral Grace must, once at least, read Luther. The Diet of
Worms is almost on us. I need instructions.

FREDERICK   Tomorrow. Tomorrow I'll read. I've just remembered,
I must—

SPALATIN   Let's read it together. "The grace and peace of God
be with us in our beginning"—

FREDERICK   Skip that.

SPALATIN   Then the dedication to the Emperor.

FREDERICK   Actually, I wanted to go hunting.

SPALATIN   "The grace and peace of God be with us in our beginning"—

FREDERICK   All over again, back to page one.

SPALATIN   Will Your Electoral Grace now—

FREDERICK   No, I will not! I want to know whether I can pocket
the Church or not. A simple question. A simple answer.

SPALATIN   With this, yes.

FREDERICK   Good. And how?

SPALATIN   We have here found a quite simple trick. We are all
priests.

FREDERICK   I'm in no mood for trifling, Spalatin.

SPALATIN   Celibacy is of course abolished.

FREDERICK   Then we might discuss it.

SPALATIN   Everyone who has been baptized is a priest. One becomes a religious as one becomes a mayor.

FREDERICK   Children, children, is that true?

SPALATIN   There's nothing against it in the Bible, and we've read
it from cover to cover.

FREDERICK   Well, fine if it's not in there. Priests then.

SPALATIN   From this it follows, if we're all priests, that we don't
need any priestly class. That's to say, the priests are superfluous,
the Roman Church with them. There's nothing left but secular
power and secular law. Ecclesiastical law we can burn.

FREDERICK   Children, children.

SPALATIN   The Bible.

FREDERICK   But how do I get at the money?

SPALATIN   Ah—there we've dug up an old theory of emergency.
If the Church doesn't do her duty, it's the task of the worldly
power to reform her. If it's the worldly power that fails, well, it's

true that then the Church may intervene. But we have deleted this second half. And we have made the emergency rights of higher authority into a duty of authority.

FREDERICK   There's something to be said for an emergency like that. So I'll reform the Church. But how do I get at the money?

SPALATIN   For that we've printed a small special treatise. On the Babylonian captivity of the Church. And here we prove that there are really only two sacraments: baptism and communion.

FREDERICK   And the rest?

SPALATIN   Are superfluous. There's nothing about them in the Bible. And that makes all our beloved priests and monks jobless. For what is there left for them to do if nearly all the sacraments are eliminated? They'll have to go. And that makes all Church benefices, revenues, and foundations free. The property of the Church can be devoted to other purposes.

FREDERICK   And to prevent this lovely money falling into un-righteous hands I take it into my own, for I am a Christian Prince and have the right and the duty to reform the Church. And no-body can take it amiss, for I am also a priest. Made to measure, I call that.

SPALATIN   Your Electoral Grace has an excellent understanding of the matter.

FREDERICK   And, what's more, it's religion!

SPALATIN   None but religious questions.

FREDERICK   Yes. All just a question of the packing. How much do you weigh?

SPALATIN   A hundred and sixty-three pounds.

FREDERICK   That's too much for me. How old?

SPALATIN   Thirty-six.

FREDERICK   Then you will get on every birthday as many golden guilders as you are years old. I hope in your own interest that you grow old in my service.

SPALATIN   Your Electoral Grace is too kind.

FREDERICK   I know. But supposing someone says, "That's all wrong."

SPALATIN   God's word. As believing Christians we keep strictly to God's word. And as is well known, it is difficult to do any-thing against God's word.

FREDERICK   And the Pope?

SPALATIN   We've of course made exceptions.

FREDERICK   Oh, we can make exceptions?

SPALATIN   But of course. The Pope can stay. So can the cardinals.

FREDERICK   That's good. So we've got them out of the firing line.

SPALATIN   There will be exceptions too for the nobility. The prebends, for instance, can be kept to provide institutions for the sons of princes.

FREDERICK   That'll please the fathers. Have you thought of.. Charles?

SPALATIN   We emphasize that the Kingdom of Naples belongs not to the Pope but to the Emperor.

FREDERICK   He'll be pleased. And Fugger?

SPALATIN   All church fairs and pilgrimages are abolished. All holidays except Sunday are eliminated.

FREDERICK   That will please him.

SPALATIN   Moreover, people are to work more and gorge and tipple less.

FREDERICK   That'll make him downright happy.

SPALATIN   Then a few nice things are said about the universities. We need these gentlemen. Something against usury, for the knights. A bit of poor relief for the people. First we have to say something to everybody. Then we can sort things out.

FREDERICK   Isn't this too revolutionary?

SPALATIN   Not at all. It's conservative. We take the money, the rest have God's word.

FREDERICK   And the common folk?

SPALATIN   Will be urged to lead hardworking, unassuming, honest, and God-fearing lives. Moreover they are to obey the authorities and eat their bread in the sweat of their brows. Is that what you call revoltuion?

FREDERICK   Not really.

SPALATIN   Then I may submit the books to Your Electoral Grace. *(He gives him the books)*

FREDERICK   Now supposing one or other of the gentlemen won't join in?

SPALATIN   I cannot imagine that a prince would have anything against these writings.

FREDERICK   But supposing one of them wants to dance to the Roman tune.

SPALATIN   That doesn't matter. We have indeed made all these changes possible, but changes don't have to be made. Everything *can* go on as before. It's all one. Just as Your Electoral Grace pleases.

FREDERICK   I don't have to make changes?

SPALATIN   No.

FREDERICK   But if I will, it is my holy duty to expropriate the Church.

SPALATIN   Yes.

FREDERICK   So it's a pure question of faith?

SPALATIN   A pure question of faith.

FREDERICK   Well, if that is so, we'll pray God then to give us the true faith.

SPALATIN   Regarding Worms, has Your Electoral Grace anything definite in mind for Luther?

FREDERICK   Oh yes. I know various gentlemen who have long been searching for the true faith. (*He gives the books back to* SPALATIN) You may read me these on the journey to Worms. With all their prefaces. (*Both go off*)

FOOL   (*in a piping voice*) Jesus loves me, this I know. For the Bible tells me so. (*He goes off*)

TABLE LEFT FRONT

(SPALATIN *gives* LUTHER *a document*)

LUTHER   The imperial ban?

SPALATIN   Only the threat of it. The Prince wants a strong rejoinder.

LUTHER   The affair should be passed over in silence. Otherwise the ban one of these days will achieve validity just because of our exaggerated concern. The best thing is to let the matter alone. It will then die a natural death.

SPALATIN   The Elector wants the rejoinder in two versions, Latin and German. The Latin version very strong please for the scholars. The German milder. We don't want to disturb the people still further.

LUTHER If you wouldn't press me so hard, I would now commend the whole business to God and not take another step.

SPALATIN We are now preparing the Worms business. You will probably appear before the Diet and will not recant. Exact instructions will follow.

LUTHER Can I be burned?

SPALATIN More likely the others will burn first.

LUTHER For myself I fear nothing. God's will be done. I rejoice with all my heart to suffer in so good a cause.

SPALATIN All the better.

LUTHER Therefore I shall write to the Emperor that I have no intention of appearing.

SPALATIN What?

LUTHER If it's only to recant.

SPALATIN I don't understand.

LUTHER But, my dear Spalatin, it's just as if I'd already been in Worms and had returned to Wittenberg. I can save myself the journey. As for recanting, I can do that here.

SPALATIN Do you want to recant?

LUTHER No, no. Be assured I shall not recant a syllable. But it is my greatest wish that the Emperor should not stain with my blood the beginning of his reign. For it is well known how the Emperor Sigismund was pursued by calamities after the murder of Huss. Nothing went right for him any more. He died without heirs, his grandson perished, his name became extinct in one generation, his wife became a whore. And a great deal else. I hope the Emperor knows that.

SPALATIN Are you going to recant or not?

LUTHER Yes.

SPALATIN What do you mean, *yes?*

LUTHER Yes, of course. You can put your complete trust in me. *(Pointing to the document)* I shall write that the bull is forged.

SPALATIN It is genuine.

LUTHER One can then argue better. *(He is about to go off)*

SPALATIN Heh. And Worms?

LUTHER   God's will be done.

SPALATIN   Yes or no?

LUTHER   If the Emperor wants to kill me, of course I'll come. Although I had rather it was the papists who had my blood on their hands.

SPALATIN   My dear Doctor, I must deeply disappoint you. Neither the Emperor nor the Pope is after your blood, nor anyone else.

LUTHER   There, you see, Spalatin. Put not your trust in princes. All vanity and men's work. I expected nothing different.

SPALATIN   I will inform the Prince.

LUTHER   I humbly beg his electoral grace and favor and promise to continue obedient in all humility.

SPALATIN   But you won't go to Worms?

LUTHER   Who says so? If the Emperor summons me, then it comes from God. And God's word I must obey, even against your will.

SPALATIN   Against my will?

LUTHER   Yes. Then I must go to Worms, even if it does not suit you. God is my witness that I am willing and zealous to obey the Emperor. Be it to live or to die, for honor or shame, for good or ill. There's nothing to determine. Therefore I beg the Prince to procure from the Emperor for me a safe conduct and that I be not persecuted and condemned.

SPALATIN   You'll get money, counselors, a guard, imperial safe conduct.

LUTHER   Not on my account please; it doesn't matter to me. After all, it isn't my cause, my dear Spalatin. At stake is the welfare of Christendom and the German nation.

SPALATIN   That goes without saying.

LUTHER   But you distress me, Spalatin. So does the Prince.

SPALATIN   How so?

LUTHER   You have heard and understood God's word and you cannot without everlasting perdition gainsay it or forsake it. We must take care that you are not numbered among those who betray God's word. (*He bows*) I pray for the Emperor, for the Elector, for my well-beloved lords and sovereigns. (LUTHER *goes right*)

(SPALATIN *sits down bewildered on a step*)

FEILITZSCH   (*entering and giving* SPALATIN *a letter*) News from
Worms. Everything cleared up with Luther?

SPALATIN   Yes. No. That's to say, I think so. Well, in any case,
God's word.

FEILITZSCH   Something the matter?

SPALATIN   I don't see my way clearly, but it has to do with God's
word. (*Both go off*)

TABLE RIGHT FRONT

LUTHER   Once again there's a rejoinder due. I'll tear the papists'
bull to shreds about their ears.

MELANCHTHON   I should wait a little first.

LUTHER   Yes. It's what I should prefer too, to let things take their
course. But we have others to consider.

KARLSTADT   Conference with Spalatin?

LUTHER   I know you have something against the court.

KARLSTADT   Remember you began this work in the name of Jesus
Christ.

LUTHER   Well?

KARLSTADT   It could all too easily end in the name of the Prince.

LUTHER   You take a wrong view of this, Karlstadt. If I negotiate
with the Prince, it's only because they, by doing me a service,
are serving the word of God and thereby being saved themselves.

KARLSTADT   That's the view I take too.

LUTHER   There's no disputing with you. Incidentally, I'm going to
Worms.

MELANCHTHON   Are you mad?

LUTHER   Yes, that's the way I am. I have set my mind on it, so I'm
going. I know, Melanchthon, a great martyrdom awaits me, but
for myself I have no fear.

KARLSTADT   I should be going there too if I were going to find so
many friends there. Hutten and the Knights' Party. Frederick and the Princes' Party. The Citizens' Party. On the streets
the dear good People. Hosannah.

LUTHER   You won't sour my martyrdom for me. Not you. You have
absolutely no idea of true greatness.

KARLSTADT   You're right there. I am only a simple fellow.

LUTHER   We shall triumph over Pope and Emperor. We shall defeat and despise the princes. And now I'm going for a beer. I invite you both. *(To KARLSTADT)* Even you.

MELANCHTHON   Have you money?

LUTHER   I've had some earnings. Fifteen thousand altogether.

MELANCHTHON and KARLSTADT   What?

LUTHER   I've given away half of it already. I fear that, little by little, God wants to reward me. I have also told them, plain and forthright, either I give it back at once, or I shall squander it.

MELANCHTHON   Did you give it back?

LUTHER   No. So I must squander it. *(He laughs. All go off)*

PLATFORM RIGHT

(Music. On the stage people are gathering for the Diet.)

CHARLES   *(lounging in an armchair)* This stupid Diet.

MARGARET   We'll soon be on our way back home.

CHARLES   Woms. Woms.

MARGARET   Worms.

CHARLES   Worms. Worms. I'm already quite melancholy.

MARGARET   My little one.

CHARLES   And my head! Ever since I was in Germany I've had this pressure in my head.

MARGARET   That only comes from that silly crown. *(She takes the crown off his head. Moistens a handkerchief with scent and lays it on his brow)*

CHARLES   Oh, Aunt. I should so much like to be a great man. How does one become a great man?

MARGARET   We'll manage it yet.

CHARLES   Fame and honor. A man must do something great. What, doesn't matter. Some heroic deed or other. A man must think of posterity. I want to hand down my name worthily.

MARGARET   A war would be best.

CHARLES   Charles V, Charles V. What is it to be the fifth Charles? Charles the—Something must come after that, something tremendous. Charles the—Look, Aunt. My beard's growing already.

MARGARET How pretty.

GATTINARA *(coming onto the platform)* Am I disturbing you?

CHARLES You and your papers. I want to wage war. All day we sit around here signing treaties. It stinks.

GATTINARA Before war God, I'm afraid, has put treaties.

CHARLES Give me a horse, give me a banner, and I'll lead the peoples into everlasting war.

GATTINARA The peoples maybe, but not the princes.

CHARLES Oh these German princes! I'll attack them first.

GATTINARA That I would not advise. You should only begin a war where you are stronger.

CHARLES Words of wisdom.

GATTINARA You have no money and no soldiers.

CHARLES I have lands.

GATTINARA And that is all you have.

MARGARET *A propos* lands. I'd quite forgotten. I have a surprise for you, baby.

CHARLES Let me guess. Hm. I've got it. Hm. No I have that. What can it be?

MARGARET I've bought you Württemberg.

CHARLES Württemberg. Yes. Württemberg. How nice of you. Where is it, then?

MARGARET In the direction of Switzerland. Come. Make a nice bow.

CHARLES *(bowing)* I welcome my Württembergers. Who paid for it?

GATTINARA Fugger.

CHARLES Amazing fellow. Seems to have money.

GATTINARA To balance it, Spain is as good as lost.

CHARLES What you build on in front, he seems to lose behind. Perhaps you can make an arrangement between you.

MARGARET If we hadn't bought Württemberg it would have fallen to Switzerland. They'd have pushed out all authority there and by today all Germany would have been one single republic.

GATTINARA Madame overestimates the Swiss. It would be better to worry about Spain. I mean, otherwise we'll have a democracy there.

MARGARET Spain is your department.

GATTINARA   Madame insisted on coming to Germany.

MARGARET   The boy only wanted his crown.

CHARLES   What are you arguing about?

MARGARET   Politics, my little one, politics. Just don't get excited. (CHARLES *puts the crown on his head*) Now leave that thing off your head. It only gives you a headache.

CHARLES   It's my crown. Gattinara, your treaty.

GATTINARA   Things are bad in Spain. Civil war.

CHARLES   I bear it with kingly detachment.

GATTINARA   We have evidence that the Pope is behind it.

CHARLES   Filthy swine.

GATTINARA   The King of France is taking advantage of the situation to attack in Spain and Holland.

CHARLES   Another filthy swine.

GATTINARA   We must act. I propose that we attack the French in Milan. If we hold Upper Italy, we have all Italy, and France will have lost an important position.

CHARLES   Against the Pope and against the King of France? What was that you said just now? Something about attacking only where you're stronger—

GATTINARA   Allies, that's the stateman's answer. The German princes must supply us with soldiers and the Pope must fight on our side.

CHARLES   And how do we bring that about?

CATTINARA   Well, first of all I'd give Fugger a nod; that always helps. And then I'd concern myself very intensively with that Luther.

CHARLES   That stupid monk?

GATTINARA   He belongs to the Princes' Party. The Knights' Party is in with them too, and so are the citizens. And the Curia trembles at the mere mention of his name. Here is a letter from our Rome ambassador. He recommends us to take Luther into our favor. With his sermons we can cause the Pope great difficulties.

CHARLES   Luther is an important man.

GATTINARA   And that's why we must use him. Uncle will be bringing him to the Diet with him. Even if we wanted we couldn't prevent that. Therefore let us send him an official invitation. By this means we can hint to the Pope that perhaps there's a religion more useful to us than his. Once half Europe believes in Luther we no longer need to march to Rome. We'll be carried to Rome. Just see how quickly the Pope comes over to our side.

CHARLES   Good. Send a message to the Pope that if he causes confusion in my affairs I'll bring him into a confusion that he won't easily get out of. He is to take his hands off Spain immediately. Moreover, I want a pact of aggression with him against France.

GATTINARA   A defense pact.

CHARLES   We want to attack.

GATTINARA   It's called a defense pact.

CHARLES   All right, then. A pact for defense, mutual assistance, and friendship. And spread a report that Luther wants to send me a hundred thousand men whose burning wish is to march on Rome.

GATTINARA   It shall be done immediately. *(Is about to leave)*

CHARLES   Gattinara.

GATTINARA   Charlie?

CHARLES   Couldn't we get Luther over to us?

GATTINARA   We're already working at it. *(Goes off)*

CHARLES   *(pointing to the crown)* Look, Auntie, it doesn't press any more.

PLATFORM LEFT

(FUGGER kneels at his prie-dieu, rosary in hand, and prays.)

SCHWARZ   *(coming onto the platform)* News from Worms. Charles wishes you to come.

FUGGER   I am used to my debtors coming to me.

SCHWARZ   Perhaps, however, you ought—

FUGGER   The Diet has to meet in my house; if the young gentleman wants to introduce new fashions, let him do so. He will see where that gets him.

SCHWARZ   We must have a talk with him about his debts.

FUGGER   How much is still outstanding?

SCHWARZ   Sixty million. (FUGGER *crosses himself*) Forty million we're supposed to get out of Austria. That may be possible. But twenty million in Spanish state loans.

FUGGER That's possible too.

SCHWARZ I should refuse them, waste paper they look like becoming. Who knows who'll be governing Spain tomorrow?

FUGGER Charles will. I'll give him a few cannons. That'll settle matters. And charge him eight per cent.

SCHWARZ We give the Emperor a preferential rate.

FUGGER Exactly.

SCHWARZ Maximilian paid five.

FUGGER He came to Augsburg.

SCHWARZ Won't you go to Worms personally, after all? Charles has great schemes.

FUGGER Great schemes cost money, and money is here. Just let the little man run up debts. A great mass of debts. I'll worry about the accounting. And block the Papal Nuncio's account.

SCHWARZ There's a hundred thousand just paid in by the Pope. For bribes—*douceurs* against Luther.

FUGGER And that we'll block too. Without the money the Nuncio won't achieve much in Worms.

SCHWARZ Do you believe in Luther?

FUGGER I believe in money and good business. Did you write to the Pope?

SCHWARZ All as you instructed.

FUGGER Let us pray God to interpret our figures in the right way, then we shall soon have a holy war again.

(SCHWARZ *goes off.* FUGGER *prays on*)

PLATFORM RIGHT

POPE The question of faith is just a joke to all of them. Luther's the fool they need to play the game. Let us join it, then. Frederick uses him, Charles uses him. Let us use him too.

CAJETAN You're the Pope.

POPE I have debts with Fugger, eight million, and can't even pay the interest. I've already had to give him my most valuable ring. If he were now suddenly to give me a credit of twenty million I should have to take it.

CAJETAN A credit with which to buy German mercenaries.

POPE   The main thing is to get the money first.

CAJETAN   Do you really want to ally yourself with Charles?

POPE   Have I any choice? If he allies himself with Germany, they'll be here in two weeks. Charles alone is bad enough. But Charles and Germany—that would be our death sentence.

BIBBIENA   They're quite capable of putting in a General Council and putting us out.

POPE   They must not unite. On no account. Charles must put Luther under imperial ban. Without further ado. Then we have them in two different camps, and Germany is divided.

BIBBIENA   And though Charles then will be standing at our gates, he will have in his rear the German princes with Luther. And that will give us all kinds of possibilities of stoking up hell for him.

POPE   If need be I'll quash the bull. A German national church as in France, why not? I see land. We ought to be downright grateful to this Luther.

BIBBIENA   Luther, savior of the Roman Church and the Pope.

POPE   So write to Charles, if he puts through the imperial ban and outlaws Luther, he'll get his treaty against France. Not otherwise.

CAJETAN   The Pope as patron of the German Reformation.

BIBBIENA   We'll be canonizing Luther yet.

POPE   Only, he must not recant. *Gloria Patri et Filio et Spiritui Sancto.*

ALL   Amen.

POPE   My blessing he has. *(All go off)*

(CHARLES, GATTINARA, MARGARET, FREDERICK, *and* the PRINCES *in the center of the stage)*

FOOL   *(in his piping voice)* Jesus loves me, this I know. For the Bible tells me so.

(Everyone claps politely)

CHARLES *(to* FREDERICK) Very nice, Uncle dear, *extraordinaire.*

FREDERICK   I thought let's have some civilized entertainment for once. Instead of all this tippling.

CHARLES   *Extraordinaire.*

(FREDERICK *nods. The* FOOL *presents* CHARLES *with a bunch of flowers*)

FOOL   Oh young and noble German blood,
                Oh Charles, great Emperor,
                Peace give us as our highest good,
                God save our Emperor.

ALL   Hurrah, hurrah, hurrah.

CHARLES   Very sweet. How you called?

FOOL   Nickie Fool.

CHARLES   Herewith I open plenary session of German Diet. Uncle dear, you, I, talk later.

FREDERICK   Undoubtedly.

(CHARLES, GATTINARA, *and* MARGARET *go to platform right.* FREDERICK, ALBERT, *and some* PRINCES *go to platform left.*)

PLATFORM LEFT

ALBERT   *(on the way to the platform)* I say, this Luther writes here you want to ban the brothels.

FREDERICK   Does it say that there?

ALBERT   Here. *(Showing him the passage)*

FREDERICK   One is never told the important things.

ALBERT   Are these the kind of swine's tricks you're up to? Just when I'd got my brothel properly going again.

FREDERICK   We can make exceptions.

ALBERT   I should certainly hope so.

(*A* WAITRESS *brings beer mugs onto the platform*)

THE PRINCES   Ah. *(They drink)*

ALBERT   Do you know this one? A bishop comes naked out of the confessional—

FREDERICK   Gentlemen, let's be civilized, I beg of you. On parade! (*The* PRINCES *form themselves into a men's choir,* FREDERICK *as conductor*) Your voices. (*The* PRINCES *practice their voices*)

THE PRINCES   *Lalala mimimi wowowo* (etc.)

FREDERICK   *(rapping for silence with his baton)* Gentlemen, this time it's the real thing. So all with one voice, if I may so advise. I'm listening.

1ST PRINCE   Nothing for the people.

2ND PRINCE   Nothing for the knights

3RD PRINCE   Nothing for the citizens.

4TH PRINCE   Nothing for the Emperor.

5TH PRINCE   Everything for us.

FREDERICK   And the property of the Church?

ALL THE PRINCES   We'll pocket it ourselves.

FREDERICK   Everyone keeps in good voice. Luther appears before the Diet. One for all. All for one.

2ND PRINCE   Will he hold out?

FREDERICK   Leave me to take care of that.

3RD PRINCE   He mustn't become too popular with the people; that wouldn't be good.

FREDERICK   He'll soon be unpopular.

ALBERT   I'm against.

FREDERICK   Against what?

ALBERT   Luther.

FREDERICK   I told you that exceptions can be made.

ALBERT   Against it.

FREDERICK   Shit.

ALBERT   Shit yourself.

(FREDERICK *takes a beer mug and brings it down on* ALBERT's *head.* ALBERT *falls*)

1ST PRINCE   But gentlemen. Be civilized.

(ALBERT *gets up hastily.* FREDERICK *takes the next beer mug*)

ALBERT   I was always for Luther, from the begining.

FREDERICK   *(putting down the beer mug again)* A nice tuning fork.

1ST PRINCE   All for one. One for all. There's nothing better than Luther after all.

2ND PRINCE   I've already borrowed four million on the security of the Church estates.

3RD PRINCE   Yes, and I've only got my debts deferred by pawning the Church estates. If I can't collect them, I shall be in the hands of the receiver.

4TH PRINCE   If Luther recants, we'll have to go into liquidation. So what do you want?

ALBERT   *(shouting)* But I only have Church estates! If you expropriate the Church, I can go begging. I'm a Cardinal.

FREDERICK   I've said one can make exceptions.

ALBERT   Well then, how?

FREDERICK   Luther will think of something. You can explain your case to him.

ALBERT   And if he can't think of anything?

FREDERICK   He'll think of something. Give you my word. It's all theology, and that's why it's possible.

ALBERT   You could have said that straight away. Well then, all together. *(He raises his hands)*

1ST PRINCE   Heavens, when I think that this evening I shall be out of debt. (FREDERICK *conducts*)

PRINCES   *(singing)* Here are we gathered for praiseworthy deeds. . . .

PLATFORM RIGHT

GATTINARA   We need six thousand light horse, two thousand heavy horse. Thirty thousand foot, fifty guns with cannoneers, powder, and two hundred cannonballs apiece. And sappers.

CHARLES   When does the war begin?

GATTINARA   Not war. A campaign of pacification. We are going to liberate Italy.

CHARLES   And when?

GATTINARA   As soon as we have pacified Spain.

CHARLES   My first war.

GATTINARA   It's like your first wife. You get used to it.

CHARLES   The women are already hanging round my neck.

(MARGARET *gets up and goes out*)

GATTINARA   That with the women wears off. A man's wars stick to him.

"Wars are for the veteran
Nature's greatest gift to man."

CHARLES   Why war?

GATTINARA   Why?

CHARLES   Yes. Why?

GATTINARA   I should have to think about that.

CHARLES   Do so.

GATTINARA   Admittedly, you can lose a war. It costs a lot of money. The countries are exhausted. But what sort of arguments are those, I ask you? After all, it is the Emperor's duty to win fame and honor. It wouldn't be understood if there were no more war. It is expected on all sides. Your subjects would be disappointed and would think very badly of you. They want to sacrifice themselves for you. And besides, you stand for a good cause.

CHARLES   What cause?

GATTINARA   Your own! God Himself is on your side and it would be actually tempting God to bring in here a simple peace. No, no, peace is blasphemy. My dear boy, you make me quite confused.

CHARLES   I promised peace.

GATTINARA   There you have the tensions between ideals and that self-interest which in the case of a sovereign is so entirely justified. The King of France is even allying himself with the Turks to wage war, and they are infidels.

CHARLES   And we?

GATTINARA   We ally ourselves with the Persians.

CHARLES   Why?

GATTINARA   They're the enemies of the Turks.

CHARLES   And infidels.

GATTINARA   Yes.

CHARLES   But behind them, are there more enemies and infidels?

GATTINARA   The world has not yet been completely explored. But the system must undoubtedly be capable of development.

CHARLES   Shit of a statesman.

GATTINARA   I beg your pardon?

CHARLES   What does the Pope say?

GATTINARA   He'll supply sixteen thousand foot and he offers you

the crown of Naples. If you proscribe Luther, everything's
straightforward.

CHARLES   If I proscribe Luther I shall get not one penny or one
soldier out of the Princes.

GATTINARA   A so-called diplomatic stalemate. So a summit conference is due. Your first big job, Charles.

CHARLES   From today "Your Majesty."

(GATTINARA *bows*—FREDERICK *and* CHARLES *come down
off their platforms.* SPALATIN *and* GATTINARA *follow their
masters*)

FREDERICK   I'll diddle the lad.

CHARLES   I'll diddle the old buffer.

(They go up to one another and embrace)

CHARLES   Uncle!

FREDERICK   Charlie!

*(They sit down on two chairs by the footlights. Behind them
stand* SPALATIN *and* GATTINARA)

FREDERICK   How's everything?

CHARLES   Well. Well.

FREDERICK   How's your aunt?

CHARLES   Old. *(Pause)* Uncle. I problem statesmanship.

FREDERICK   So have I. I have another three millions coming from
you.

CHARLES   Yes.

FREDERICK   Money. Three millions.

CHARLES   Fugger.

FREDERICK   Fugger says Charles.

CHARLES   Fugger. (FREDERICK *gets up*) Uncle, not be angry.
(*To* GATTINARA) Uncle, three millions. (GATTINARA *bows*)
Yes.

FREDERICK   I'm listening.

CHARLES   I money.

FREDERICK   Luther is appearing before the Diet.

CHARLES   I soldiers.

FREDERICK   Demands of the Knights' Party and of the people are being suppressed.

CHARLES   I ally of Pope.

FREDERICK   All power is with the Princes.

CHARLES   Luther recant?

FREDERICK   No.

CHARLES   Good. But I Luther imperial ban.

FREDERICK   What happens in Germany is decided by us.

CHARLES   We talk figures?

FREDERICK   We talk figures?

CHARLES   How much money? How many soldiers?

FREDERICK   No money, only soldiers. Since your late grandfather once boozed away the wages for a hundred-thousand-man army, we no longer make deliveries except in kind.

CHARLES   You imperial government Germany. I vote in favor.

FREDERICK   We don't give a hoot for your favor.

CHARLES   Uncle dear. I Emperor.

FREDERICK   Elected by us. Elected by me.

CHARLES   Emperor.

FREDERICK   If you get up to any tricks you won't grow old in the job.

CHARLES   I keep face.

FREDERICK   That we thoroughly understand. We are ready to recognize you as supreme head and to support you accordingly, but Germany belongs to us.

CHARLES   And Luther? Pope wants edict, otherwise I no war.

FREDERICK   What can we do about this?

SPALATIN   The Emperor can issue the edict of outlawry only with the approval of the representatives of the nation. If that is of any use.

FREDERICK   That is of use. Charlie, what about this? Soon after Luther's appearance I'll get an attack of gout and go back home. My friends will leave too—without gout. That'll deprive the Electoral College and the Diet of a quorum, and you can issue any decree you want. They'll all be invalid.

CHARLES   Pope knows too when Diet shut.

GATTINARA   There I would suggest a small correction. We'll backdate the edict. To a day when the Diet still had a quorum.

FREDERICK   Certainly, if you please. It is in any case invalid since it won't have lain before the Diet and consequently cannot be taken up into the prorogation minutes and will therefore lack legal force. Moreover I suggest you don't even send me the thing, for what should I do with invalid papers? It only clogs the administration.

CHARLES   You at least read.

FREDERICK   What I don't have in front of me doesn't exist for me. I know of no edict. Otherwise I should find myself ultimately in the embarrassing situation of having to prove to the public that you had signed an illegal edict.

CHARLES   Good. Wastepaper basket. But Luther also go underground.

FREDERICK   Shall be attended to. *(They get up and embrace)*

CHARLES   Uncle!

FREDERICK   Charlie!

CHARLES   Luther not recant. Clear?

FREDERICK   Everything clear.

CHARLES   He thinks he's going to diddle us.

FREDERICK   He thinks he's going to diddle us.

TABLE RIGHT FRONT

CHARLES   This Luther's a handy weapon. If one could have it in one's hand.

GATTINARA   One can't get at the man himself, Your Majesty. Frederick sees to that.

CHARLES   I have a sort of idea. Isn't another Council due?

GATTINARA   Overdue, Your Majesty.

CHARLES   The Pope wouldn't like a Council, would he?

GATTINARA   It's worse for him than the plague. The Council, you see, could depose him and elect a new Pope.

CHARLES   A pope who does what I want. Who doesn't dictate any more treaties to me.

GATTINARA   A Council would be a splendid thing.

CHARLES   We must get Luther on to our side. You can earn yourself an order.

GATTINARA   I already have them all.

CHARLES   Then see that you keep them.

TABLE LEFT FRONT

FREDERICK   Is Luther here at last?
SPALATIN   Just arrived.
FREDERICK   Resolute?
SPALATIN   Not very. He's suddenly got every kind of illness.
FREDERICK   Don't let him be unguarded for a minute.
SPALATIN   I've detailed a hundred men for the job. The house in
   which he lives is occupied by us. Two of our best people lie in
   the same room with him.
FREDERICK   See they don't sleep.
SPALATIN   If I may advise you, you must now go some way to meet
   him. He's afraid.
FREDERICK   His time in any case has run out. He has done his work.
   Very nicely, very well. We'll take him prisoner. Tell him that
   I will hide him if he does not recant. Take a few good men. On
   the journey home stage a mock hold-up and bring him to a safe
   place.
SPALATIN   He's always had this longing for a castle. We could put
   him in the—
FREDERICK   No names. Nothing. I know nothing. I haven't a clue.
SPALATIN   But we could—quite independently of the Luther ques-
   tion—discuss the merits of your castles.
FREDERICK   Yes, we could do that.
SPALATIN   For instance I would say the Wartburg was a very fine
   peaceful castle. Nothing but woods round about, few people,
   good cells. In short, for anyone who wants to go into retreat,
   ideal.
FREDERICK   I agree with you. But I know nothing about Luther.
   I swear before Almighty God that I have nothing to do with this
   affair.

TABLE LEFT FRONT

(*During the following scenes everyone slowly moves to the rear.
They stand there with their backs to the public, on the platforms*

as well. At center stage a corridor is kept free. LUTHER *enters. There is polite applause.* GATTINARA *approaches him.)*

GATTINARA   My dear Doctor. I am a great admirer of your books.

LUTHER   I'm glad.

GATTINARA   Yes indeed. Very interesting treatises. Here and there a few exaggerations, but I imagine one could discuss those—couldn't one?

LUTHER   I am ready for anything. I've always said so, Your Worship—pardon me—your title?

GATTINARA   Of no consequence. We're all men.

LUTHER   I should be so glad— Here I can't—

GATTINARA   I understand. *(He takes him aside)* In case you're afraid of your Saxon friends, I know of a rich benefice for you, hard by a castle and under the protection of the Emperor. We could easily reach agreement there. There are so many possibilities. There we should be guided entirely by your wishes. What do you think, for instance, of a General Council of the Church?

LUTHER   I have been demanding it for years.

GATTINARA   Wonderful. We could then depose this dreadful Pope and discuss your books in peace and quiet.

LUTHER   I should be ready to stop writing. At once.

GATTINARA   Well, look at that now. You're unjustly reputed to be such a devil of a fellow. You're not the man they take you for.

LUTHER   If only that were realized, Your Excellency. I should like—

SPALATIN   *(approaching)* What's the subject?

GATTINARA   The weather.

SPALATIN   Interesting topic.

GATTINARA   Yes. I think it's going to rain.

SPALATIN   *(to* LUTHER*)* Is that what you think too?

LUTHER   *(bewildered)* I don't know.

SPALATIN   May I have a word? *(He takes* GATTINARA *aside.* PEUTINGER *sidles up to* LUTHER*)*

LUTHER   Dr. Peutinger.

PEUTINGER   My dear Doctor, the things you're doing! Have you considered the matter at all?

LUTHER   How do you mean?

PEUTINGER   Do you intend to hand Germany over to these butchers? You're only filling their pockets with your sermons.

LUTHER   I keep to the Bible.

PEUTINGER   You and your Bible. You can find anything you want there. You get rid of the infallible Pope and nail us to an infallible Bible instead. The Pope can be changed. A book can't. You must recant. What is to become of this country? Two religions. Every man against every other. Didn't you ever read Erasmus? And the princes will be the first to begin the slaughter.

LUTHER   I really don't know any more.

PEUTINGER   I tell you these gentlemen will bless us with a Germany fit to make our hair stand on end.

LUTHER   I can't change it.

PEUTINGER   Who else?

LUTHER   My dear Doctor. I am only one of the very little ones of my party. Others are much more important. Nothing at all would come of it if I recanted, because the others, who are so much more than I and so greatly surpass me in learning, would still not be silent. They would carry on the cause despite me. (*He looks at the ground. He wipes his eyes with his sleeve.* SPALATIN *comes up and pushes* PEUTINGER *aside*)

SPALATIN   The weather?

PEUTINGER   I think it's going to rain. (*He goes off*)

SPALATIN (*to* LUTHER)   It would be better if you didn't have so many talks. Or you'll find the rain heavier than you bargained for. The Elector's annoyed as it is that you didn't come at once. Contrary to your assurances.

LUTHER   I was—

SPALATIN   You were hanging around in Wittenberg another week although you already had the imperial safe conduct.

LUTHER   I wasn't feeling well. I'm ill.

SPALATIN   Tell that to your doctor. Have you your instructions?

LUTHER   Yes.

SPALATIN   Good. If you recant, I can no longer guarantee your life. (LUTHER *nods*) Off with you. (*Some armed men take* LUTHER *in their midst and conduct him through the free corridor to the rear.* SPALATIN *follows.* WINDOWCLEANER *enters humming a song*)

FOOL   Secret session.

WINDOWCLEANER   I only wanted to give the windows a clean. Are they all inside already?

FOOL   All with any business there.

WINDOWCLEANER   How can they see clearly if they can't even see the light of day? They must let the light in. Everything bright and clear so that you can see through it. Is Luther inside too?

FOOL   He's facing them.

WINDOWCLEANER   Then they'll soon get going. At last a man who dares to give the high-ups a piece of his mind.

FOOL   (telling it off on his buttons) He will recant. He won't recant. He will recant. He won't recant. He will recant. He won't recant.

WINDOWCLEANER   He won't recant. Not he. He's entirely on our side, and that's a thing the gentry there will notice. If they're in there, the north wing should be free still. I'll try there. (He goes off singing. A disturbance; some PRINCES and GENTLE-MEN come forward)

1ST PRINCE   Time to consider! He's asked for time to consider. Time to consider! (LUTHER is conducted onto a platform by the armed men. People try to persuade him)

FREDERICK   (coming forward, roaring) Spalatin! Spalatin! (SPALA-TIN dashes to his side) Is he mad? Has he gone out of his wits? What does he think he's playing at? My reputation. Time to consider. Why is the fellow here, then? Does he want to put me to shame? If he doesn't immediately—

SPALATIN   I'll see to it. (Goes off)

CHARLES   Uncle, what what? How I stand before Pope?

FREDERICK   Give you my word he won't recant.

2ND PRINCE   I'm ruined. I'm ruined.

3RD PRINCE   I'm more than ruined. There's never been such a bankruptcy.

FREDERICK   Gentlemen! Keep calm. Always consider that you are the first men of Germany. Compose yourselves. Don't think of your debts, think of your great names.

(CHARLES and the PRINCES go back to the rear. LUTHER too is conducted to the rear by the armed men. He comes past FRED-ERICK. They stop a moment. FREDERICK scrutinizes LUTHER *from head to foot, then points curtly to the rear.* LUTHER *is taken away.)*

SPALATIN Won't you come too?

FREDERICK I am not concerned in the affair.

(SPALATIN *goes off rear.* FREDERICK *remains standing in front. The* WINDOWCLEANER *dashes on from the left)*

WINDOWCLEANER *(shouting)* I'm the windowcleaner. Stupid pack. Clean your windows yourselves. (*To* FREDERICK) A whole week I've been trying to clean the north wing. Every day it's secret session. And you? D'you have business with them too? (FREDERICK *nods)*

WINDOWCLEANER Clerk? Confidential clerk? I'm the windowcleaner. (*Shakes* FREDERICK's *hand)* Brandy? *(Pulling out a bottle)*

FREDERICK No thanks.

WINDOWCLEANER My own making. *(Drinking out of the bottle)* Is Luther still inside? (FREDERICK *nods)* Luther's all right. He's the only one who occasionally thinks about the likes of us. He's wholly on our side.

FREDERICK Is he popular?

WINDOWCLEANER What a question! Of course he's popular. Look out of the window. The streets are full of people. And placards everywhere. Down there look they've just set up one from the peasants. Eight thousand men who want to protect Luther. Yes, yes, times are changing. Here in the newspaper it says the same. There. A turning point in German history. Dawn of the new age. Everything will be different. Everything will be better. Everything will be nicer. Now begins the merry-go-round. An end of authority. Princes, Church, away with it all. Aren't I right, friend?

FREDERICK Yes indeed.

WINDOWCLEANER And that I say although as a windowcleaner I'm a conservative sort of man.

FREDERICK Why so?

WINDOWCLEANER It's always the same. Soon as something's up they smash the windowpanes. Thoroughly stupid habit. . . .

Well, I'll have a look if the south wing's free today. Although it's probably no longer worth it. (*Goes off right. A disturbance. Some of the Princes confer with* CHARLES. SPALATIN *plunges forward*)

SPALATIN   First, he has written nothing but Christian books which he has no need to recant. Secondly, polemics against the Pope, those he will be glad to change. Thirdly, disputations about the faith. Disputations do not need to be recanted. Fourthly, he asks for instruction. If he is in error, he will recant. Fifthly, he summons the Emperor to war.

FREDERICK   Bribed?

SPALATIN   He's trying to extricate himself.

FREDERICK   Place him beside me.

(FREDERICK *and* SPALATIN *go off rear. The circle closes up again. The* WINDOWCLEANER *plunges onstage from the right*)

WINDOWCLEANER   (*roaring*) I'm the windowcleaner! God blast and confound it! They'll be saying afterwards the window panes they smashed at Worms were dirty. Where's my friend then, the confidential clerk?

FOOL   That was the Prince of Saxony.

WINDOWCLEANER   Holy smoke! (*He has another drink out of his brandy bottle*) That's the way it is with us folks, always standing on the wrong leg to shout hurrah. Is Luther still inside?

FOOL   Yes.

WINDOWCLEANER   He's taking a long time just to say no.

(*From the assembly shouting and applause*)

WINDOWCLEANER   (*calling out*) He hasn't recanted. Ready steady go. Smash the windowpanes. (*Goes off*)

(*The* PRINCES *come forward.* CHARLES *and* FREDERICK *bow to each other*)

FREDERICK   (*loudly*) Charlie, I'm leaving for home.

CHARLES   (*loudly*) Already? Bad news?

FREDERICK   The gout. I'm in such pain, unendurable.

CHARLES   I'm sorry. Bon voyage.

(FREDERICK *goes off*. CHARLES *turns around. A* CARDINAL *comes to meet him.* CHARLES *hands him a document. The* CARDINAL *hands* CHARLES *a document. They bow to each other. Both go off. Out of the background the masses of the people roll forward. They carry* LUTHER *on their shoulders. Placards, signboards:* Down with the rulers. Power to the People. Luther, the German Titan. Luther, the hero of the people, *etc. Shouting, huzzaing.*)

LUTHER   *(roaring, beside himself)* Murder and blood! Murder the bishops! Destroy the monasteries! Kill them! Root them out! Wash your hands in their blood! Be God's loved ones! Insurrection! Insurrection!

(The people roar back. Curtain)

Two

"THE SWORD OF GOD"

(The Curtain rises)

PLATFORM RIGHT

(The front steps have been drawn up. LUTHER is sitting at a table, writing. He is wearing trousers, jacket, boots, and a full beard. Silence. Two soldiers come with breakfast. They let down the steps and march onto the platform).

1ST SOLDIER *(saluting)* Wartburg Tower First, Squire George Bodyguard, taking over day watch.

1ST and 2ND SOLDIERS Good morning, Squire Goerge.

LUTHER Good morning, friends.

1ST SOLDIER Beg to report, your breakfast.

2ND SOLIDER May I ask if Your Honor had a good night, or was Your Honor again obliged to wrestle with the Devil?

LUTHER With the Devil, my son, quite dreadful. Three times he was here during the night. *(The SOLDIERS sit on the ground)* First it creaked and groaned everywhere.

1ST SOLDIER The rafters.

LUTHER No, no, the Devil. Then all of a sudden *hoo hoo.*

1ST SOLDIER The wind.

LUTHER No, the Devil. Then I suddenly hear him in the passage, as if he were dragging a heavy sack into Hell.

(The SOLDIERS laugh)

2ND SOLDIER With the sack, that was Andie.

LUTHER But I went on sleeping and that angered him greatly. And all of a sudden on the stairs a clatter, as if barrels were thundering down the stairs.

1ST SOLDIER It nearly crushed me.

LUTHER I rushed out and onto the stairs. Nothing.

1ST SOLDIER I only just got away.

LUTHER Then I called out, "Is it you, so be it," and went back to bed. *(The SOLDIERS laugh)* Then he did come into my chamber. Threw my nuts onto the blanket, shifted table, chair, my bed, so that I almost fell out of it. But I commended myself to God, turned my back on him and farted in his face. Then he finally left me in peace. That's the best remedy. It's the only way to get rid of him. Stink against stink. (*The* SOLDIERS *roll about laughing*) What are you laughing about? You'll soon stop laughing if he drags you off into Hell.

2ND SOLDIER   Couldn't you act Luther again for us?

LUTHER   I did it only yesterday.

1ST SOLDIER   It's Bartel's name-day and he wants you to do it for him because you saw Luther in Worms. What does he look like?

LUTHER   Well, like this. So you want me to act him for you?

2ND SOLDIER   Yes, but properly, from the beginning, with his entry.

LUTHER   Good, then I'll play you the real Luther. So, he comes into the hall—something like this. (*He makes a few big strides toward them*)

1ST SOLDIER   Yesterday you came from the other corner.

LUTHER   Right. The door was here. (*He goes back*) So he came from here. (*He makes a big stride*) No, the door *was* there. Ah well, it's all the same, so I come in. (*He makes a few strides and strikes an imposing attitude just in front of the* SOLDIERS) Then I looked about me, quite slowly. So he stood there, as I stand before you now, and looked around him. In the hall it became quite quiet. Everyone turned pale. There where you're sitting now there sat the Emperor. And there, Frederick of Saxony. And round about only princes and knights. I stood here. Steadfast.

2ND SOLDIER   And Luther?

LUTHER   He too. He was standing. The Emperor looked, Luther looked, everyone looked. Quiet. From over there someone looked across. (*The* SOLDIERS *laugh*) And then the Emperor said he wasn't going to make me out a heretic. Then says Luther, "And with pounding hammer I have nailed the theses for you to the doors of the century and I have thrown the Ban of Empire into the flames of the century, and here I stand, I can do no other." (*No longer in his pose*) Then I was given another mug of beer and in the Wartburg I smashed the ink bottle against the wall. The stain can still be seen. That is the true Luther. (*He sits down again. The* SOLDIERS *laugh and applaud.* BERLEPSCH *comes up the steps. The* SOLDIERS *jump up*)

1ST SOLDIER   Bodyguard Squire George on guard. Nothing special to report.

BERLEPSCH   Withdraw. (*The* SOLDIERS *march off*) Stop acting Luther so often. The people are sharp enough as it is to know what's behind it all.

LUTHER   They're too stupid to notice anything.

BERLEPSCH   It's I who am responsible. If something happens to you the Prince will hang me.

LUTHER   The Prince is a man you can talk to.

BERLEPSCH   You as a theologian perhaps. I am a captain. You have God's word in your pocket and can always talk yourself out of trouble. All I have are service regulations. And they will hang me. Bowels moved?

LUTHER   Not for five days.

BERLEPSCH   We all have our trials. If it doesn't take you from the rear, it takes you in front. For me it's with women, doesn't work any more. Busy?

LUTHER   I'm translating the Bible into German.

BERLEPSCH   Into German? We have that already. You can buy them on every street corner.

LUTHER   My printer thinks that now I have a name it would be good business.

BERLEPSCH   I hope he's right. My cousin's a librarian in Nuremburg. He's got whole shelves full of German Bibles. Whole shelves full, I tell you.

LUTHER   They're all worthless. I have one here. (*He opens it*) It's bad. Very bad. Here it reads—

BERLEPSCH   I understand nothing of it. Are you coming hunting with me? Some hare?

LUTHER   Why kill hares when so many enemies of Christendom are still alive?

BERLEPSCH   It's a point of view, certainly. Have you heard about Karlstadt?

LUTHER   What?

BERLEPSCH   He's going to get married. A fifteen-year-old. Cuddlesome.

LUTHER   Whoremonger.

BERLEPSCH   You could too, now.

LUTHER   I? Marry? Never! They won't saddle me with a wife. I stay a monk. That'd be the last straw, the monks leaving their monasteries and getting married.

BERLEPSCH   But your monastery is said to be nearly empty already. The monks have all left it.

LUTHER   *(banging his fist on the table)* So that they can stuff their fat bellies and go after women. Why don't I hear all this till afterward? Don't even think fit to ask me.

BERLEPSCH   One of my officers was in Wittenberg for Christmas. Home leave. He told us that Karlstadt had abolished the Latin mass, everything without all that ceremony, no chasubles, no confession or communion in two kinds. They say that is the evangelical mass.

LUTHER   And such a thing calls himself a priest. He's messing up the whole religion for me.

BERLEPSCH   But I thought that was now all permissible?

LUTHER   Permissible. Permissible! That would just about suit those gentlemen. Do as they please. Everything permitted. Without asking me. Who was it then who stood up to Emperor and Diet? Who fought for freedom? Here I put my life at stake, and those gentlemen introduce reforms. If I'm killed—

BERLEPSCH   Doctor, for heaven's sake, don't cause trouble for me. If the Prince were to hear that! You're as safe here as in Abraham's bosom. Drawbridge up, tower steps up, everything according to regulations. And only hand-picked men. Here nobody goes in or out except at my orders. And my orders I receive from the Prince. The mere idea that you could be in mortal danger here is a thing I should wish not to have heard.

LUTHER   Something must be done at once. A tract must be published. Have a messenger ready; I must send Spalatin a tract.

BERLEPSCH   Do you want to write against it?

LUTHER   Against it? For it. For it. Away with the mass, away with the monk's vow.

BERLEPSCH   For it?

LUTHER   If anyone is to change anything here, then it must be I. I am Luther. *(He sits down and writes)*

BERLEPSCH   Well, I'll go after the hares. *(He goes off)*

TABLE LEFT FRONT

MÜNZER We must do it ourselves, Karlstadt. They won't do it for us. The godless must be cleared out of the way, so that the righteous may have time and space. It is not possible for a man to think under this tyranny. All Germany slaves so that a few lords may feast. People are waking up. They do not want to be oxen drawing a show-cart. They have been told they're animals and suddenly they notice they're men. I was in Zwickau with the clothmakers. I was in Joachimsthal with the miners. Now I've been in Prague.

KARLSTADT Prague?

MÜNZER Yes. I wanted to try something from Prague. The Bohemians know a thing or two about revolution.

KARLSTADT And?

MÜNZER Expelled.

KARLSTADT As usual. You've been everywhere, Münzer, and everywhere they've expelled you.

MÜNZER It doesn't worry me. I'm used to it. On the contrary, if I'm not expelled after three days I become suspicious—begin to think there's something wrong with my preaching.

KARLSTADT No no, lawful reforms. Step by step. Nobody can object to that. Here. The draft of our new order, the municipal code. We establish a common fund. All ecclesiastical revenues now come into this fund. An inventory is drawn up of the valuables belonging to the monasteries and churches.

MÜNZER So that you may find them later in the princely treasuries.

KARLSTADT Wait. The fund is administered by two city councilors, two municipal representatives, and a clerk. Nobody is to go begging any more. The poor, the sick, and the orphans receive support. Gifted children receive a grant so that they may study. The rest are to learn a trade. Artisans without means and poor people receive short-term credit, free of interest. If anyone is deeply in debt and has heavy interest to pay, the fund takes over the discharge of his debts. For this he pays into the fund only four per cent interest. Surpluses can be used to procure city supplies—corn and the like. If there's too little money, every citizen, each according to his property, must contribute something. Then we must see about new teachers, the priests receive three-quarters of their previous revenues as salary, and in general we provide that the mass to be held here is the evangelical mass.

MÜNZER Will you get it through?

KARLSTADT The council is for it and so are all the inhabitants.

MÜNZER And the Prince?

KARLSTADT It is all according to law. Peace and order. A vote in the council. The Prince must see that.

MÜNZER But the prison's already full?

KARLSTADT He can't lock up the whole town.

MÜNZER I think an expulsion will soon be due. Travel light, if I may advise. Heard anything of Luther?

KARLSTADT A short letter. He's afraid of people looking for him. We are in God's name to keep our mouths shut. He says it's for the honor of Christ.

MÜNZER Where is he?

KARLSTADT No idea. A secret special operation. Not a soul knows anything.

MÜNZER Where could he be?

KARLSTADT How should I know? Somewhere or other. Above the clouds. Directly beside God.

MÜNZER On Whose right hand he will sit.

KARLSTADT If we now change the mass—

MÜNZER —it'll make not the slightest difference to the people.

KARLSTADT It does make a difference.

MÜNZER Yes, I do see, it's part of it. Property is defended by God's word, therefore it must be attacked with God's word.

KARLSTADT *(with a manuscript)* I have a problem here.

MÜNZER *(reflectively)* It should be put into German so that they understand it. So that they see through the great mummery. A German mass. I shall write a German mass. Have you some money for me? Only if you can spare it. (KARLSTADT *gives him a piece of money)* I'm going to Allstedt. There are miners there.

(Goes off)

PLATFORM LEFT

(FREDERICK *has a document in his hand*)

FREDERICK   *(tearfully)* So these are the sort of resolutions they pass here. Resolutions like these in my lovely Wittenberg. Is that gratitude? Spalatin, is that gratitude?

SPALATIN   Your Electoral Highness, it is not gratitude.

FREDERICK   When I'm always so gracious to everyone. Like a father to his children. Anyone can do what he wants with me. If he observes my rules. *My* rules. *(He reads)* Municipal code of the city of Wittenberg. This is insurrection, revolution. I'm robbed of speech. Have I deserved this? Have I deserved this, Spalatin?

SPALATIN   Your Electoral Highness has not deserved it.

FREDERICK   *(reading)* The goods of the Church will be distributed to the poor. No, no, no! I won't even read such blasphemous stuff. To the poor. What should they do with all that money? The poor are the poor, that's why they're called poor. That's what makes the world go round. Why must people always be thinking about money before everything? I am most deeply disappointed.

SPALATIN   Your Electoral Highness will know how to console himself.

FREDERICK   Oh, this world! I am quite depressed. A prince like me is only human. People never think of that. Municipal code. Just at this moment, when I'm taking over the presidency of the imperial government. What am I to say to my colleagues? Shall I say the Church estates are for the poor? My capital city confiscates everything for itself while I look on? My very bones will be put to shame. I shall be the laughingstock of all Germany. I shall no longer be called Frederick the Wise but Frederick the Dupe. It would mean that we should never have started the business with Luther. I put my strength behind the man and when I come to collect the cash, my subjects have already emptied the till. It's against all nature.

SPALATIN   Your Electoral Highness can forbid it.

FREDERICK   I do forbid it. I absolutely forbid it. What happens with the Church estates is for me to decide. For me alone. My advice to the city council. If it is not followed, then there'll be a counting of heads. And then I'll hold a lottery. And what's that here about the mass? *(He reads)* German. Evangelical. What's this?

SPALATIN   Karlstadt has reformed the mass.

FREDERICK   Didn't I forbid that?

SPALATIN   Strictly.

FREDERICK   And he's done it all the same?

SPALATIN   All the same.

FREDERICK   Prison.

SPALATIN   Your Electoral Highness, the people will set fire to the castle.

FREDERICK   There you have it, rebellion. Revolution. And with that I'm supposed to take over the imperial government? With revolution in my own country? The other gentlemen will thank me for that. Spalatin, I give you two weeks. When I take over the imperial government, absolute quiet must reign here. Municipal code out of the way, mass out of the way, Church estates at my disposal. I will have a model state. Everything can be read about, disputed, and preached about, but everything remains just as it was. Nothing is to be changed.

SPALATIN   Your Electoral Highness, then we need Luther.

FREDERICK   Why, he's as bad as anyone at beating the big drum!

SPALATIN   He's been shut up for ten months; it's made him soft.

FREDERICK   What'll the other lords say if I let him out?

SPALATIN   If he gives us peace and quiet, nothing. After all, it's all in the lords' own interest. And a man like Luther you only get once. You see what happens when he's removed. The people all at once have thoughts of their own, and they are not at all to our taste. New men come on the scene, and they preach not only against the Church, they preach against us. If they once get a foothold—

FREDERICK   But I must not have anything to do with it. Nothing. Nothing at all.

SPALATIN   We can operate from behind the city council and the University. If we then let it be seen that things won't work without him.

FREDERICK   I want a letter from him. For the imperial government. A letter in which he writes why he is coming back to Wittenberg, that he is coming against our will and without our knowledge, that he will observe moderation in all things, that he will not be a burden to anyone, and please phrase the letter so that I can lay it before the government.

SPALATIN   If you will then just sign this.

FREDERICK   What is this?

SPALATIN   The order or release.

FREDERICK   Must this be?

SPALATIN   I should not wish my head to be counted.

FREDERICK   Pedant. *(He signs)* When will he be here?

SPALATIN   In a week.

FREDERICK   My goodness, what a surprise I shall have.

(SPALATIN *goes off*)

TABLE LEFT FRONT

LUTHER   Can I take the mask off now?

SPALATIN   Yes. Have you the letter for the Prince? (LUTHER *gives him the letter. He takes off the beard and puts on a cowl. SPALA-TIN quickly scans the letter. He laughs*) Very prettily phrased and very courageous. But you must rewrite it once more. That cannot be laid before the imperial government. I'll send you a new draft.

LUTHER   Thanks, I can write myself.

SPALATIN   Copying is safer. My dear Doctor, the Prince wants quiet in his state. Quiet and then again quiet. The things that have been happening here recently do not accord with our ideas. All day long the people have been running through the streets— meetings, plebiscites, disputations, speaking choruses from morning to evening. You could no longer have a proper chat or read a good book in peace. It was horrible.

LUTHER   The folk have every reason to snatch up their pitchforks. The way they're oppressed and ground down in this state.

SPALATIN   One Karlstadt is quite sufficient, thank you. The Prince wants a quiet, obedient, and industrious population. And above all, no changes.

LUTHER   Always only preaching and changing nothing; it was hardly necessary to start the preaching in the first place.

SPALATIN In certain circumstances you might find yourself back in the Wartburg quicker than you would like.

LUTHER Why didn't you keep me better informed? We should have intervened much sooner.

SPALATIN I seem to remember you didn't want a too frequent correspondence, so that your hiding place should not be betrayed.

LUTHER And where are my letters, my manuscripts which I sent out from the Wartburg? Nothing has arrived. Nobody's seen them.

SPALATIN We have held them back.

LUTHER What? I demand that my manuscripts be printed. At once.

SPALATIN Two of them we can discuss. If everything remains quiet. But the polemic against Cardinal Albert will not be printed. The Prince has made friends with him.

LUTHER It will be printed.

SPALATIN *(emphatically)* It will not be printed.

LUTHER And though I plunge you, the Prince, and everyone else into disaster, I wish it to be printed. (SPALATIN *keeps an icy silence*) Very well, then, it will not be printed. What does it matter? *(He nestles in his cowl)* This here is all in rags too.

SPALATIN I see that once again you need a new cowl. But this time the city council will pay for it.

LUTHER Unfortunately I can't eat it.

SPALATIN The Prince will pay you a starting salary of—let's say —twenty thousand a year.

LUTHER And where shall I be living?

SPALATIN In the Augustinian monastery. It's standing empty and awaits a new master. It would be opportune perhaps if you could explain to the city council that its new municipal code is not according to the will of God. The gentlemen, you see, want to confiscate all Church estates and give them to the poor. Then the Augustinian monastery too would go, and it's a fine rich living.

LUTHER It seems that God's word has been stirring up a lot of confusion in the heads of the common folk.

SPALATIN Yes. And If I may advise you, keep yourself somewhat in the background. The public should get the impression that you want to live a retiring life.

LUTHER Disputations I suppose are allowed?

SPALATIN   Disputations, yes. So long as the people are not disturbed by them.

LUTHER   Have no fear. The people will get their proper sermon. (SPALATIN *goes off.* LUTHER *goes right*)

TABLE RIGHT FRONT

MELANCHTHON   Luther. *(They embrace)*

LUTHER   My dear Melanchthon, you see how from sheer necessity I have plunged into the raging seas of Pope and Emperor in order to drive the wolf from my fold. Unprotected, surrounded by enemies, my head bare to Heaven.

MELANCHTHON   I have found a quiet room. As you wanted. You can live there in hiding.

LUTHER   Christ's thoughts I know not. But I do know I was never so courageous as I now am.

MELANCHTHON   Now we shall really get going.

LUTHER   Yes. And to prevent you backing the wrong horse, it is God's will that everything should now go into reverse.

MELANCHTHON   Into reverse?

LUTHER   Yes. It seems that I always have some particular danger to surmount. First Augsburg, then Worms, now Wittenberg.

MELANCHTHON   But you said you agreed with everything.

LUTHER   Did I say that?

MELANCHTHON   How will you make this clear to the people?

LUTHER   My dear Melanchthon, we have so often spoken about faith, about the hope for that which is not seen. Why cannot we for once make a trial of this teaching? It is done at God's command and not according to our will.

MELANCHTHON   I don't understand.

LUTHER   We shall do best to keep the middle of the road. Let me be reproached with treachery because I listen to the Prince, or cursed for playing a double game. I assuage my conscience by telling myself that it is the usual way of behaving.

MELANCHTHON   The people will be indignant.

LUTHER   You are right. I have made concessions enough. Now at

last there is need of some free speech. (LUTHER *goes off left.*
MELANCHTHON *stays behind in bewilderment*)

TABLE LEFT FRONT

(KARLSTADT *is sitting at the table working. On the table a
Bible and manuscripts*).

KARLSTADT   Why, look, our martyr.
LUTHER   *(coming to the table)* A little while, and ye shall not see me;
and again, a little while, and ye shall see me. *(He sits down)*
Where's your fifteen-year-old?
KARLSTADT   Warming my bed.
LUTHER   Strange things we hear about our lovely Wittenberg.
KARLSTADT   What, for instance?
LUTHER   Everything a bit topsy-turvy.
KARLSTADT   For the court it was topsy-turvy. We enjoyed our-
selves and found it all very orderly.
LUTHER   Rebellion, violence, revolt.
KARLSTADT   Says the court. I say, no rebellion, no violence, no
revolt.
LUTHER   And the iconoclasts?
KARLSTADT   That was your dear brother monk, Zwilling. It wasn't
going fast enough for him.
LUTHER   What have you made of Wittenberg? It was a peaceful
little town. We preached, and the people were grateful. Today
every stupid peasant accosts you and puts questions. The glorious
freedom of the children of God, what's become of it?
KARLSTADT   We had the freedom to take freedom for ourselves.
LUTHER   Religious enthusiasm.
KARLSTADT   When we lay claim to freedom, then suddenly there's
no longer any freedom there for us. Then all at once we hear
"Backward march, march!" A misunderstanding. That isn't what
was meant. The time is not yet ripe. Radical excesses. Too pre-
mature, too hasty, order, order, my dear children. Take thought,
in Heaven's name.
LUTHER   Are you in favor of rebellion?

KARLSTADT No. I hate rebellion, as you well know. I have forbidden all rebillion.

LUTHER There you are, then. There must be order.

KARLSTADT Yes. Only question is whose order. Here, that is our order. *(He gives him a document)* Municipal code of the city of Wittenberg. Resolved by the council and citizens of this city. Voluntarily. Without compulsion.

LUTHER *(tearing up the paper)* Hereby revoked.

KARLSTADT If you're so much in favor of order, you could at least have read it. For there it is written that in this city a German evangelical mass will be held.

LUTHER Hereby revoked.

KARLSTADT Everything as in the good old days. Confession and communion as hitherto, chasubles, hymns, all the ceremonies—

LUTHER —and Latin.

KARLSTADT Weren't you once in favor of changes?

LUTHER We're not without resources even so.

KARLSTADT How then?

LUTHER I imagine the priests can silently utter a few words. That way you can hold an evangelical mass without the people noticing anything.

KARLSTADT Those of course are radical changes. The authorities notice nothing because they don't go to church, and the people notice nothing because they don't know Latin.

LUTHER You take this all much too seriously. It doesn't matter how one takes communion, whether one confesses, fasts, stays in the monastery or not. None of it has any significance. Divine service. A theater show with sermons for the people.

KARLSTADT And the revenues of your people's theater? The property of the monasteries, the Church domains, that has no significance either?

LUTHER Of course not.

KARLSTADT How gratifying for the princes! Our municipal code says that it belongs to us all.

LUTHER Don't talk to me about your municipal code. What I need is in the Bible.

KARLSTADT That too is only a book.

LUTHER   God's word.
KARLSTADT   A book.
LUTHER   God's word.
KARLSTADT   It is a book, written, printed and sold by men.
LUTHER   It is God's word for all eternity.
KARLSTADT   Greetings to the new Pope.

LUTHER *throws the Bible at* KARLSTADT. KARLSTADT
falls, gets up again, Bible in hand)

KARLSTADT   Take care, Luther. With this book men can be killed.
LUTHER   You take note of that.
KARLSTADT   Tomorrow I shall preach that—
LUTHER   You will not preach here any more.
KARLSTADT   Good. Then I'll write—
LUTHER   You will not write here any more either.
KARLSTADT   Must I leave Wittenberg?
LUTHER   God's will be done.

(KARLSTADT *throws the Bible at* LUTHER. *He catches it and
throws it back.* KARLSTADT *dodges it. The Bible falls to the
floor*)

KARLDSTADT   Shall I tell you what you really think?
LUTHER   Tell me then.
KARLSTADT   You'd sacrifice every word of your Bible if you could
only stand at our side.
LUTHER   *(throwing manuscripts at him and roaring)* You shit!

(KARLSTADT *goes.* LUTHER *stamps with his foot just short of
the Bible*)

PLATFORM RIGHT

(*While* LUTHER *preaches, a crowd gathers in front of the platform*)

LUTHER   Must Must, Free Free, Must Must, Free Free. Dear brethren,
what have you done? Out of that Must you've made a Free and
out of the Free a Must. You have misled your brethren to free-

dom. To a loveless freedom. The mass you have abolished. Not as though that were not good, but where then is order? If authority had been joined with you in this, we should know that it happened by God's will. I should then have begun it too. For only that which happens by authority is not to be considered rebellion. Therefore have respect for authority. So long as it does not step in and give orders, you should keep still with hand, mouth and heart, do not stir. If it does not will, neither should you will. But if you go on, you're already in the wrong and much worse than the Devil. You have done wrong to begin this affair without my orders and without my help, without asking me about it first. *(The people murmur)* Yes indeed, you ought to have asked me. I wasn't so far away.

A MAN   Where were you, then?

LUTHER   You could have reached me by writing. Look at me. I have done more damage to Pope, bishops, parsons, and monks with my mouth alone than all the emperors, kings, and princes with all their power. And why? Because it was God's word. That worked while I slept or drank the beer of Wittenberg with my friends. Therefore, dear brethren, follow me. I have never yet betrayed our cause. I was the first to be put here by God. I was the one to whom God first revealed Himself, bidding me preach such words to you. And I cannot run away, I must stay so long as God wills it. It is not our work. Another man it is who turns the wheel. There are many things I could begin too and be sure that not a few would follow me. But what help would that be? What would you think of it if I set the people in movement, I who was the first to drive on others, and then wanted to run away myself? How the poor people would be misled. Therefore take note of the persons who preach to you. They are of two kinds. There are many who will not listen but mislead and poison others with their lying mouth. Therefore let us with speaking and writing hunt down this deception among the people, until it is laid bare to all the world, and so recognized and put to shame. Seek out only its malice and its godless nature will soon be destroyed. It needs nothing more than to be sought out and recognized. For nobody is so mad as not to hate lying and falsehood in public.

God give us all to live as we teach and to turn our words into deeds. Heaven is of iron, the earth of brass; no beseeching will help any more.

(He goes off. The people stand bewildered)

PLATFORM LEFT

(SPALATIN *reads out a letter to* FREDERICK)

SPALATIN   If Your Electoral Highness had faith, he would see God's glory, but since he has no faith, he has seen nothing yet.

FREDERICK   *(laughing)* From Luther? What does he write?

SPALATIN   Your Electoral Highness must be obedient and let the Emperor have power in your lands and not oppose him.

FREDERICK   *(laughing)* Has he any further pieces of advice?

SPALATIN   His heart has ever taken great pleasure in Your Electoral Highness, especially in Your Electoral Highness' famous good sense.

FREDERICK   Oh, how nice.

SPALATIN   He comes to Wittenberg, incidentally, under a much higher protection than that of Your Electoral Highness. (FREDERICK *laughs*) Nor does he want your protection. Indeed, he wants to give Your Electoral Highness more protection than Your Electoral Highness can give him. (FREDERICK *laughs*) And if he knew that Your Electoral Highness wanted to or could protect him, then he would not have come. (FREDERICK *laughs from his belly*) Your Electoral Highness is still weak of faith, and for that reason Your Electoral Highness is in no wise the man who could protect him. (FREDERICK *rolls about with laughter*) He hopes nonetheless, since Your Electoral Highness is of such high birth, that Your Electoral Highness will not act the beadle for the other lords to punish him.

FREDERICK   *(laughing)* The fellow's really too comic. *(He laughs)* —I should never have come—*(He laughs)* I'll make him my court fool. (*He points to his* FOOL) And you'll take over the Church.

FOOL   *(drumming on his chest with his fists)* Here I stand. My faith. I have. I shall. I am. My word. Oh God. *Dominus vobiscum. Habemus ad Dominum.*

(*All go off*)

PLATFORM RIGHT

(SCHWARZ *at his bookkeeping.* Three GENTLEMEN *sit round a globe.* FUGGER *mounts the platform.*)

SCHWARZ   Special shareholders' meeting of the firm of Jacob Fugger.

FUGGER   Praised be Jesus Christ.

ALL   For ever and ever, Amen.

FUGGER   This is a globe, gentlemen. Made by our good friend Behaim. God created the world and gave it out of his exceeding goodness the form of a globe. *He strokes the globe)* Round and handy. So that it can be circumnavigated by ships and trade be plied. New lands, new business. Italy, the whole Mediterranean becomes unimportant. Big business comes over the great oceans.

SCHWARZ   Point 1: India.

FUGGER   Gentlemen, Europe needs spices. Spices are obtained from India. By the overland route. But that is unimportant since a Master Vasco da Gama has discovered for Portugal a direct route to India. By sea. You certainly remember the great stock-market crash. Lisbon delivered at half the price, and the Portuguese since then have had the spice monopoly.

2ND PARTNER   But we participate.

FUGGER   I don't want participation. I want the monopoly. So I need my own route to India. And since the earth, as our scientists assert, is round, it must be possible to reach India not only from this side but also from that. Our good customer Charles, among other things ruler of Spain, thereupon had the inspiration of sending a certain Magellan on his travels. Gentlemen, what shall I tell you? The earth is round.

2ND PARTNER   Has the fleet returned?

FUGGER   Two weeks ago. The scientists are right, and we have our private route to India. We only have to lay our hands upon it quick enough.

3RD PARTNER   But my dear Master Fugger, the risk. All the things that can go wrong. Strange lands, strange seas, the ships can sink. It's all a gigantic speculation.

FUGGER   The Portuguese operate with profits up to a thousand per cent. There's room there for the loss of a few ships.

2ND PARTNER   What does this Magellan say?

FUGGER   He, I'm afraid, says nothing more. He stayed behind where the pepper grows.

2ND PARTNER   Desertion?

FUGGER   A native arrow.

2ND PARTNER   Savages.

3RD PARTNER   How big was the fleet?

FUGGER   Five ships and two hundred eighty men.

3RD PARTNER   And what came back?

FUGGER   One ship and eighteen men.

3RD PARTNER   You see.

FUGGER   I admit it's a pity about the ships, but the cargo of one ship was enough to turn the whole enterprise into a profit. Consider too, please, that in India, as generally in the whole Orient, we have a gigantic market for our copper. A market which we can now supply directly. So we earn twice over.

SCHWARZ   Point 2: America. (*He gives* FUGGER *a sheet of paper*)

FUGGER   The statistics of the gold and silver deliveries from America. They are steadily increasing. In the long run this could endanger our European market. We must therefore insert ourselves there. We need in America our own mines, best of all, without more ado, our own colonies. As it is we have the best engineers and artisans. So the rest are dependent on us. Unfortunately the Indios are not able to stand up to our progressive production methods for long. Despite the introduction of a midday break they die like flies. The few who still survive are wanted by the Folk Museum. Thank heaven the Negroes have proved more durable, and Negroes it is well known are delivered f.o.b. to the African coast. Now it so happens that our brasswares find a good market in Africa and are very much in demand. Thus we shall sell our brassware in Africa, the Negroes we shall sell in America, the American gold and silver we shall bring to Europe; in return we shall sell our copper in India, and bring back the India spices to sell in Europe. Gentlemen, this globe is precious. We shan't let it out of our hands. We shall buy and sell and thus keep it turning.

1ST PARTNER Business worth millions.

FUGGER Business worth thousands of millions. Charles meanwhile is heavily in debt to us. We'll present him with the bill.

1ST PARTNER And China?

FUGGER We have an interest in the China trade. But I'm holding back a little. I have some anxieties about that country.

2ND PARTNER I have some anxieties about the quality of our spices.

FUGGER Schwarz.

SCHWARZ Spices are stored on principle in damp cellars so that they become heavier. Ginger is eked out with brick dust. Pepper with dung, best of all mouse dung if it can be got. Saffron—

2ND PARTNER For heaven's sake. Isn't that dangerous?

FUGGER We can mix an *Ave Maria* in with them.

2ND PARTNER And if somebody dies of it?

FUGGER Everybody must die some day, and you find the profit satisfactory, don't you?

2ND PARTNER Entirely.

FUGGER Anything else?

1ST PARTNER What are we delivering to the Negroes in Africa?

FUGGER Schwarz.

SCHWARZ The last order was for twenty-four thousand chamber pots.

FUGGER Gentlemen, you see, European civilization makes its way irresistibly. Praised be Jesus Christ.

ALL For ever and ever, Amen. (SCHWARZ *shuts up the account book. All go off*)

PLATFORM RIGHT

(LUTHER *stands on the steps. In front of the platform a crowd.*)

LUTHER That, you see, is the order of society, rulers, subjects, workers, artisans. These orders must exist in the world, there must be those who give orders, there must be various ranks or classes. They say the lower classes should govern themselves.

Nothing will come of that. God knows it. That's why He has instituted the various authorities. That's why He has given children their parents, because children are bad by nature. If we had no father and no mother we should have to wish that God would put wood and stone before us, so that we could call them father and mother. We ought to honor our father and mother. This honor consists in our being obedient to them. We must think them in the right in what they tell us, and keep silence and endure it however they treat us. Further we must guard our tongues in speaking to them, not use bad words to them nor insist on our rights nor scold them, but we should allow them to be in the right and keep silence even when they go too far. For if the parents are pious and act rightly, then the child's self-will is broken without remission and it must do, let be, and suffer what by its nature it would so gladly have otherwise. Even so, when the parents punish and chastize, as is seemly, sometimes even wrongly, which yet does not harm the soul's salvation.

For every person must be ruled and be subject to other persons. Therefore we see here again how many good works are taught by this commandment because by it our whole lives are subjected to other people. And thence it comes that obedience is so highly prized. Command obedience in children and subjects. God insists that it must be so. If it is not so He does not leave it unpunished. Otherwise the children would long since by disobedience have destroyed all domesticity, just as the subjects by rebellion would have destroyed all public order, because they are many more in number than the parents and rulers. That's why this good deed too is of ineffable worth. There are no better works than obedience and service toward all those who are set in authority over us. Therefore too is disobedience a greater sin than murder, unchasteness, theft, or fraud. I thank God that He has given me and all the world so good a lesson and therewith also His watch and ward. Therefore we should above all things earnestly oblige and accustom the young people to keep this commandment insistently before their eyes and if they trangress it, we should quickly be after them with the rod and enduringly impress it upon them. So should they be brought up. Whoever keeps to it shall have good days, happiness, and well-being. Whoever is disobedient shall

come to grief all the sooner and have no joy of his life. Therefore let everyone know that it is his duty, on pain of losing
God's grace, to bring up his children above all things in the
fear and knowledge of God, so that they may be of use to the
world whether in governing or wherever else there is need of
them.

In respect of this commandment more must be said too of
obedience to our superiors. For from the superiority of parents
springs and burgeons everything else. Thus all who are called
lords stand in the place of parents. What a child owed to its father
and mother is owed by all who fall under power of command.
Therefore laborers and artisans should see to it that they are not
only obedient to their lords but hold them in honor like their
own fathers and mothers. They should do everything which they
know is wanted of them, not under compulsion and reluctantly,
but with joy and gladness, for the sole reason that it is God's commandment and pleases Him above all other works. In consideration of this they should really be paying wages for the privilege
of getting lords and masters and being allowed to have such
cheerful consciences and knowing what righteous, golden works
they are to perform. If that now could be impressed upon the
poor folk, they would leap for joy, praise and thank God, they
would with decent labor, for which they get their keep and
wages besides, acquire such a treasure as those esteemed the
holiest do not have.

Whoever will not be moved by this and behave uprightly, him
we commend to the beadle and the executioner. Therefore let
everyone remember that there is no playing with God. Know that
He speaks to you and demands obedience. If you obey Him, you
are his dear child, but if you neglect it, then take misery, shame,
and grief of heart for your wages. Should not the heart leap and
melt for joy at going to work and doing what is ordered? Yet it
is a misfortune, and a miserable blindness in the world, that
nobody believes this. It is the greatest possible reproach to the
working people to be disobedient, unfaithful, ill-behaved, and
only concerned with their own advantage. If they let nothing
please them and turn insolent, let them go in the Devil's name.
The time will yet come that they'll be glad to take service for a

morsel of bread. It all comes from this that there's no order in the world.

Nobody wants to work. That's why the artisans have to pamper their journeymen. But if there were a rule that they might not leave except under orders and that nobody might take them on at other places a great loophole for evil would have been stopped up. There's no getting along with the workpeople any more. They want a lot of money and yet do nothing or do only what they want. Is that what we mean by obedience for the master's and Christ's sake? Yes, you're a devil, you're a robber, you with your lazy manner of working. It is just as bad with the artisans and laborers, who behave with such intolerable license nowadays, as if they were masters of another man's property and as if everyone must give them without further ado as much as they ask. Let such people go on asking for money as long as they can, but God will not forget his commandments and will reward their services accordingly. He'll bring them to the gallows. All their lives long they shall know no happiness and nothing will come of them.

And truly, if there were a proper government in the land, such presumption would soon be tamed and thwarted, as it once was, when such a man was quickly taken by the forelock and made an example to others. Therefore do your duty and let it be God's care to feed you and provide your sufficiency. We should raise our hands to Heaven and thank God for joy that He has given us such promises to keep us going to the world's end. But people who will serve neither on the land nor for defense, but only laze and idle, are not to be tolerated but driven out of the land or forced to work. Therefore I shall make no concessions to those who say "I am a poor man." If I knew of one who had children whom he would not allow to work, I should beg the mayor to throw him into prison and let him starve to death. I too have had much to endure and you forsooth do not want your child to work. Such poor people who live so idly should be punished. You lead a better life than the Prince of Saxony. Where will that lead? To the town filling up with beggars. And after that they'll be stealing in the gardens.

And would to God there were no holidays in Christendom and that the feasts of the saints might all be on Sunday. Then we should be spared many wicked doings, and through working on every weekday moreover the states would not get so poor. But now we are plagued with all these holidays to the ruin of our souls, bodies, and goods, for the doings which take place on them are worse than on our days of work. Idling, guzzling, tippling, gaming, and other wicked doings. Furthermore the common man suffers bodily harm twice over. For he both misses his work and consumes more than usual, weakening and maiming his body. Only the priests are to be free of work, maintained by tithes, and to have every day a holiday. There are for them no working days, but every day is like another. Therefore let nobody compel you to observe any holiday. You are free men, but free from the Devil, from death, from hell, from sin, from idolatry.

Yet you must not so understand your freedom as to say "What do I care about my master and my mistress?" That is not your freedom, that is not right for Christians, that you should be disobedient. God does not wish to break in pieces the secular order but to strengthen it. He wishes you to serve the power which is set over you with body and soul. Therefore it is necessary that this should be strongly enjoined on the great masses. They must have God's wrath always set before their eyes and drilled into their souls. That is truly a fine sermon that comes from the heart. In the sweat of thy brow shalt thou eat thy bread. As the bird to fly so is man born to work. That is a fine, golden saying of which everyone should take good note. Be assured that God cares for you. If you do not take thought, where shall I get money and lodging? Where shall I live? Work is to be done more for the service of God and the avoidance of idleness and obeying His commandments than for providing and being anxious about how a man is to be fed. For God we know will bring that about if we do our work in simplicity according to His commandment.

If we had eyes and ears, the grain would speak to us: "Be cheerful in God, eat and drink and consume me and serve your neighbor." Even so the cows: "Rejoice, we bring you butter and cheese, eat and drink." Even so the chickens: "We want to lay eggs for you." Even so I hear the pigs grunt joyfully, for they give pork and sausage. The peasants behave as if they must starve to death. They have no grateful joy in God's gifts. It is not possible that God should let anyone die of bodily hunger, sooner must all the angels come and feed him. I have been young and have grown old and have never yet seen a believing person who trusts in God forsaken or his child have to go without bread. The rich have remained needy and hungry but those who seek God do not want for any good thing. I have not, as experience shows, kept myself alive by care. The great care that peasants and workers should have is about the Devil.

We Christians are called to work and suffer; whoever will do his work rightly will have suffering enough. These two things therefore will we do. Caring we will leave to God. If anything untoward comes your way, do but suffer it gladly. This is a teaching that only we Christians have. The others do not have it. Think what a jewel it is to live quiet and peaceful in the Lord, even though the world be full of misfortune. Care not where the misfortune comes from, for God is lord of that. For such a man everything, even the worst, would be but a pleasant yoke. It is good to instill this into the common folk, that it and things like it are given by God and must be prayed for by us.

In like fashion we must speak of obedience to authority. We are obliged to honor it and to prize it highly as the dearest treasure and the most precious jewel on earth. Why do you think the world is so full of disloyalty, scandal, misery, and murder, because everyone will be his own master and free. Therefore we get as wages what we seek and deserve. Plague, war, famine, conflagration, drought, unruly women, children, and workmen and all manner of misfortune. From where should such misery come otherwise? First of all we must establish secular justice and its sword on good foundations, so that nobody may doubt that it is in the world by God's will and disposition. The sayings on which it is founded are as follows. Let every soul be subject to the power of government and authority, for there is no power which does not come from God. Power, everywhere that it exists, is ordered by God. Whoever then opposes power opposes God's order. But whoever opposes God's order will bring on himself his own condemnation. Be subject to human order of every kind. The secular government has the sword and it freely hews off the heads of mutineers. For that is the will of God.

In all things we should consider that the power of authority, whether it do justice or injustice, cannot harm the soul but only the body and goods. That also is the reason why it is not so very dangerous when the secular power does injustice as when the ecclesiastical power does it. For the poor people believe and act as they see and hear the ecclesiastical power do. If they see and hear nothing, they believe and do nothing. Therefore the ecclesiastical power is a great and exceeding good. The priests, preachers, and altogether the dear word of God and the holy Christian Church, this whole world can neither picture nor understand what a great gift it is. Therefore let the rabid princes and lords do what they will, and suffer it. The lords are lords only of money. If they persecute you, be careful not to get angry. Be through the faith kings in eternal life. It will yet come to light how things truly were with us Christians. Then will they be compelled to say "The Christians are peaceable folk." For you are lords of a lordship which is nine times greater than a hundred worlds, the lordship over sin, death, and the Devil. Let that be enough for you. Therefore Christ offers himself quite willingly to the secular government. He pays taxes, honors authority, serves, helps, and does everything He can to promote the power of government so that it may be maintained in strength and honor and fear.

For it is a work that is very useful and needful. If you were to see that a hangman, beadle, judge, lord, or prince was missing and you found yourself suitable for the work you would have to offer yourself and apply for the post, so that the power of government, which is so necessary, should not be despised and thwarted or perish. Thus it is that both go well together, that you should do justice both without and within, at the same time to the Kingdom of God and the kingdom of this world, that you should at the same time suffer ill and injustice and yet punish ill and injustice, at the same time not oppose and yet oppose evil. For in one you regard yourself and what is yours, in the other your neighbor and what is his. Thus I think is the word of Christ brought into accord with the sayings which set the sword to work. By them God breaks our will, but in the breaking of our will God's will is done. For He is well pleased when our will is hindered and made naught. So when someone wants to make a fool of you, you should not resist but say yes to it. If he wants to take something from you and do you harm, let it go. Even though the man in question were doing wrong, no wrong would happen to you. For everything belongs to God, God can take it from you by the agency of a bad man or a good.

But let no rebel interfere and suck his poison from this lovely rose and teach that the princes should be killed and authority despised and not obeyed. Of this kind are all those who, because of one injustice which happens to them or others, want to batter in the wall with their head. Let them do so. They think they are obliged and do right to get angry and straightway sound the alarm. Take note of it: It is a sure sign of bad will if a man cannot endure oppression. For where a man will let nothing please him, no good can come of it. Then come the useless babblers who fill all humanity with their talk and have seduced the poor folk with their doctrines, and cry aloud how we should have good will, good intentions, and good resolves. With this doctrine they create nothing but obstinate, self-willed people, insolent and self-assured spirits, who do not break and subordinate their own will. Their intentions, they believe, are good and must prevail. From that quarter come the most dangerous men of all. For we must give up all hope that anyone could have a good will, a good intention, a good resolve.

Now it will be objected: God has given us free will. Yes, truly he has given you free will. Why then will you make of it self-will and not let it be free? If you do with it what you will, then it is not free but your own. A free will is one that wants nothing of its own, that is why it stays free. Our will is the greatest thing about us and against it we must pray: "Oh Father, let me not reach that point that things go according to my will. Break my will, oppose my will, happen to me what may, only let it go with me not according to mine, but according to Thy will." This must reach so far that a man becomes quite lax, free and without will, and no longer knows anything but to wait for God's will. That is true obedience, such as in our times unfortunately has become an unknown thing. God sends us suffering and strife long enough to exercise a man thoroughly and make him so peaceable and quiet that he is not moved by whether it goes well or ill with him, whether he die or live, whether he be honored or shamed. There dwells only God Himself. There are no works of man any more. Therewith he demonstrates that there are no things more precious than suffering, dying, and all kinds of misfortune. And of this teaching the whole scriptures are full, full, full.

(LUTHER *goes off*)

PLATFORM LEFT

(*A crowd in front of the platform*)

MÜNZER   I, Thomas Münzer, wish you the peace to which the world is an enemy. For the innocent are tortured, and our masters do what they like with us by saying "I must torment you, Christ suffered too, you must not resist me." Therefore we must examine precisely why our persecutors of all people give themselves out to be the best Christians. The havoc of the foolish world must be recognized, in all its origins. For the truth will make all men free. Then the great man will have to yield to the small and be shamed by him. Oh, if the workers knew that, it would be of great use to them. But the peasants and workers know nothing of it, because they have put their trust in the most lying folk. Who say, oh goodness, they're work-sodden folk, they've spent their lives in earning a living. Yes, and stuffed their masters' gullets full. What should the common folk know about it? They stand outside and hope that one day things will get better.

The common folk have never had any other hope and believe to this very day the lords know what is right. They think "Eh, those are fine gentlemen in their red and brown caps, shouldn't they know what is just or unjust?" They boast of the Holy Scriptures, write and proudly splash their ink about, whole books full, and keep babbling more and more, saying we have written in our laws this and that, Christ spoke thus, Paul wrote this, the prophets have prophesied this and that, this and that the Holy Church has declared, yes a great to do, this and that. They have thrown the Bible to the common folk as you throw bread to dogs and after all know nothing about it except that it's of ancient origin. They preach what they like.

And if you seek counsel from these scholars—and you must work mighty hard beyond all bounds before they'll open their mouths, for a word from them costs many a brass farthing, and there's not one will answer you unless you give them fifty florins, yes, the best want a hundred or two and the greatest honors on earth—and if you pay and say, dear, reverend, worthy high scholar, and suchlike rubbish, then they say "Have faith, my friend, have faith, if you will not have faith, then go to the Devil." And you: "Oh most learned of all doctors, I would gladly have faith, but in what?" And they: "Yes, my friend, you must not bother your head about such high matters. Only have faith, in all simplicity put thought from your mind, it is idle fancy. Go among the folk and be cheerful, so you will forget your cares." You see, dear brother, such is the comfort that rules the world. They think folk must be told what they would like to hear, for, oh goodness, if such high teaching had to be explained to them, they would get quite rabid and frantic. Pearls must not be thrown before swine. What has such high, such entirely ecclesiastical learning to do with the poor rude common folk? It is fitting to be known only to the scholars.

Oh no, oh no, dear people, should you not be astonished what fools they have made of you? You have been deceived more shamefully than tongues can tell. They arrange it so that the poor man does not learn to read properly and they preach impudently, on top of that, he must let himself be ground down by the lords. When will he then learn? How is it possible for the common man with his worries over his daily bread to have time for reflection? They preach in their enthusiasm the scholars are to read fine books, and the workers and peasants are to listen to them. Oh yes, there they've found a splendid trick. You dear good folk, those who call you holy and virtuous are deceiving you. And those who tell you without any grounds have faith, have faith, till the snot plasters your nose, they should be speaking to swine rather than men. For everyone sees that they are striving after honors and possessions.

Therefore must you, the common man, yourself be taught, so that you may be no longer led by the nose. We are more brutal to the nobility of our souls than the irrational beasts. Not one person has an understanding of the exploitation and malice of this world. And that is why we poor miserable Christians think no more of God. Nobody will yet take it to heart; they suppose it must be hushed up. Oh the great miserable blindness, when anyone might learn to see it with half an eye. Look at the sort of folk we Christians have become. Quarreling day in, day out over money and possessions and getting more covetous every day. But you say "I believe and hold to the Christian faith and have a firm, strong hope in God." You, dear fellow, you know not what you are saying yes or no to. Yes, without doubt, you were born of Christian parents, you have never once had doubts, you want to stand firm too, yes, yes, a good Christian. Truly, they are fine people. They have indeed a firm and strong faith. But things would look prettily with us if we were to put our trust in their masquerades and babble. Look around you, you have the silliest of all the faiths to be found on earth today. And should any other man seek improvement through this faith which we still have today, a fine deal of good it would do him.

For there is no nation under the sun which so miserably abuses and curses its own law as do today's Christians. I would I could see far around me, all over the globe, inspect all nations, and many there are that I should find far superior to us. They help our brothers, we take from our brothers. Nobody is so dear to us as we ourselves. Let us mind our behavior very soon, or we shall lose our natural reason from sheer self-interest. In such blindness do we wander, we don't even want to believe anyone who tells us we are blind. Let our eyes be opened, so that we may realize our blindness. The blind lead the blind and they fall together into the pit of ignorance. We must join harmoniously together, with the people of all nations and religions; then the hidden truth which has so long slept will come to the light of day. The time of the harvest is here, dear brothers. The tares cry out in every place, the harvest is not yet they say, yet today's humankind will yet find the right impulse. That I believe.

(MÜNZER *goes off with the crowd*)

PLATFORM Right

(CHARLES *on his throne.* FUGGER *ascends the platform.*)

FUGGER   Your Majesty.

CHARLES   I need money. At once. Today.

FUGGER   You speak like your late grandfather. It's true he always was needin' coin. It sounded nicer.

CHARLES   Good. I'm needin' coin.

FUGGER   May I remind you of your truly majestic debts, Majesty?

CHARLES   Don't talk to me about old debts. Bread long since eaten.

FUGGER   Like his late grandfather.

CHARLES   Don't talk to me about my grandfather. We live in a new age.

FUGGER   With the old debts.

CHARLES   Won't you give me anything more?

FUGGER   How about the repayment?

CHARLES   There are other banks.

FUGGER   Your Majesty, if I give it out on the Exchange that you are insolvent, the loan market for you is dead. No bank will advance you a farthing.

CHARLES   You're talking to the Emperor.

FUGGER   I'm talking to my debtor. You are "Majesty" because I paid for it. That thing you wear on your head was bought for you by me.

CHARLES   (*taking off the crown and offering it to* FUGGER) Do you want it?

FUGGER   I'm not a scrap merchant.

CHARLES   (*putting the crown back on*) I can't pay. As you well know.

FUGGER   Yes.

CHARLES   So? What do you want? Pledges?

FUGGER   There's a ship of a certain Magellan just come back. Spices from India bring profit.

CHARLES   For that I need a fleet. How am I to get hold of a fleet?

FUGGER   If you transfer to me the control of the spice trade, you will have within a few months a brand-new fleet.

CHARLES   And the Spanish merchants? They see millions too.

FUGGER   Your Majesty, stop blathering! My time is valuable. I want the spice trade.

(CHARLES *looks at* GATTINARA. GATTINARA *nods*)

CHARLES   Granted, with grace.

FUGGER   You can call yourself Admiral.

CHARLES   I'd rather have money.

FUGGER   Give me your quicksilver mines.

CHARLES   The quicksilver mines? The only thing which really brings in money?

FUGGER   I would meet you in the matter of the concession price.

CHARLES   But then you will have the quicksilver monopoly as well.
(FUGGER *looks in a bored manner at the ceiling.* CHARLES *looks at* GATTINARA. GATTINARA *nods*) Granted, with favor. How much are you paying for the concession?

FUGGER   Lignum vitae is an excellent remedy against syphilis.

CHARLES   I haven't caught that yet.

FUGGER   But many other gentlemen have. There's a big market. I want the monopoly.

CHARLES   Granted.

FUGGER   How?

CHARLES   With all grace and favor. Any other monopoly to oblige? While we're at it.

FUGGER   Nothing occurs to me at the moment. But perhaps there should be a clarification in principle. A monopoly on monopolies.

CHARLES   I need money on money. My soldiers are dispersing. I want to conquer France. Once I have France, I'm solvent.

FUGGER   Good. *(He writes out a check)* Let's say forty million for the quicksilver concession.

CHARLES   Forty million?

FUGGER   Twenty million I'll keep for the amortization of your debts. Twenty million for your war against France. Is that enough? *(He holds out the check* to CHARLES)

CHARLES   Twenty million? *(He takes the check)* Won already.

FUGGER   When Your Majesty receives the news of victory, you will please sign here. *(He hands over a deed)*

CHARLES   What's this?

FUGGER   A few thoughts about monopoly capitalism. I buy you the mastery of Europe, and you preserve monopoly capitalism for me.

CHARLES   Monopoly what?

FUGGER   Like his grandfather. He never knew his way about either. But you'll get to know about it in time. *(He gets up)* I take my leave. I have another appointment. Once we have the fleet, we'll have a talk about Negroes and American colonies. *(He goes off)*

CHARLES   *(the check in one hand, the deed in the other)* Tell me, who is really master of Europe? I or he?

GATTINARA   Does Your Majesty want to know the truth?

(CHARLES takes off the crown, stuffs the deed and the check into his pockets and goes off with GATTINARA)

PLATFORM RIGHT

(LUTHER is standing on the steps. A crowd in front of the platform.)

LUTHER   Nobody ought to fight and quarrel against his lord, for we owe authority obedience, honor, and fear. For whoever aims the axe above his head, the chips will fall into his eyes, and whoever throws stones into the air, they'll fall on his own head. That is in brief the whole of the law as God Himself has ordained it.

MAN'S VOICE   Can it not sometimes happen that authority must be put down?

LUTHER   The heathen knew nothing of God, did not realize that secular government is God's order, for they thought of it as something which man through his own doing had achieved. Therefore they struck out boldly and even thought it praiseworthy when a noxious, wicked authority was put down and driven out. But it is no use to us to cite such examples. For we are not asking here what the heathen have done. Even though today or tomorrow a people should rise and put down its lords, it does not follow from that that it would be legal or permissible. I know of no case where it would be permissible. I cannot at the moment think of any. Though perhaps it may be permissible to put down a lord if he goes mad.

MAN'S VOICE   A tyrant is much worse than a madman. He does much more harm.

LUTHER   Here we must pause for an answer, because this objection has appearances strongly in its favor. But yet I say to it that the cases of a madman and a tyrant are not alike. A tyrant takes a hand in many things by his own actions. Thus he knows where he does injustice, and conscience and knowledge are present in him. Moreover, a bad example might be derived from it. If it is approved that tyrants are murdered or driven out, that will soon spread and a general free-for-all will come of it. It is better that the tyrants should do you a hundred times wrong than that you should do the tyrants wrong once.

MAN'S VOICE   And the Swiss?

LUTHER   They say the Swiss too in bygone times killed their lords and made themselves free. They gave as their reason the intolerable tyranny which the subjects had to suffer. But I have said that I am here not speaking of that which the heathen do. Till now such causes have always landed on the rubbish heap. The Swiss have already paid dear for it with much bloodshed, and we may easily guess how things will turn out there. I on the other hand see no governments more durable than in those places where authority is held in honor, as among the Persians, Tartars, and other such nations. They have not only been preserved against conquest but have destroyed many other states in the bargain.

MAN'S VOICE   Must we then put up with anything the tyrants do? You concede them too much. By such doctrine their wickedness becomes all the stronger and greater. Must we then tolerate in this wise that every man's wife and child, body and goods are delivered over to danger and shame? Who will undertake anything decent, if we must live so?

LUTHER   If you see that authority is rabid and does wrong, what matter is it to you if it ruins your goods, body, wife, and child? For it cannot hurt your soul. And it does itself more harm than you, because it brings its own soul into perdition. Don't you think enough vengeance is done on it by that? What would you do if your authority had to wage a war in which not merely your goods, wife, and child, but you yourself too for your lord's sake had to suffer disaster and let yourself be captured, burned, or strangled? Would you for that reason strangle your master? How many fine fellows do you suppose the Emperor Maximilian during his whole life lost in his wars? Yet nothing was done to him because of it. That notwithstanding, he is the real cause of their destruction because they were killed for his sake. How does a tyrant then differ from a dangerous war costing the lives of many a fine, honest, and innocent man? Yes, a bad tyrant is sooner to be borne than a bad war. That you must admit. Now choose and judge, whether you will rather have war or tyrants, for you have deserved both.

MAN'S VOICE   We want neither war nor tyrants.

LUTHER   Such creatures we are. The punishment for our sins we want to avoid, and offer resistance what's more. If authority is wicked, well then, there is God above, He has fire, water, iron, stones, and countless other means of killing. How quickly He has slaughtered a tyrant! He would do it too, but our sins will not allow it. We see it well enough when a godless man rules, but what nobody will see is that he is ruler not because of his own godlessness but because of the sins of the people. The people do not look at their own sin and think the tyrant rules because of his godlessness. So blinded, perverse, and foolish is the world. That is why you need not complain that through our teaching the tyrants and authority are made secure so that they may do evil. We do teach that they should be secure whether they do evil or good, but we cannot give and guarantee them this security. For we cannot compel the great mass of people to follow our teaching. We may teach what we want, yet the world will do what it wants. God must help, and we must teach those who would gladly do good and right that they may perhaps help to hold the great masses in check. For rebellion is directed as much at the rich as at persons in authority and in all probability we may guess that rebellion is not liked by any rich person. There is something desperate and accursed about a mob. Nobody is so good at ruling a mob as the tyrant. Were it possible to rule the great masses in a better way, then God would have set over them a different order from that of the sword and the tyrant. The sword indicates clearly what sort of children it has under it: that is to say, none but soulless miscreants.

MAN'S VOICE   But when a lord binds himself with oaths and then does not observe the constitution?

LUTHER   Well then, if such a lord recks nothing of all this—should you for that reason attack and judge him and exact vengeance? Who commanded you to do so? If a war or a quarrel should raise its head against your master, let who will wage war and quarrel. Rather suffer everything that may happen to you. The great masses that do that will soon enough find their judge. When the subjects are ripe, God condemns them to start rebellion or disobedience so that they may be soundly trounced over the head. For God has entirely destined the subject person to be and remain on his own and has taken the sword away from him. For this reason if he bands himself together with others and takes up the sword, then he is guilty before God and deserving of death.

If they rebel and rise in revolt, then it is right and proper to wage war against them. And because there are among the soldiers some who feel themselves aggrieved by the ruling class and all that goes with it, so I myself have heard such fellows say, "Come to think about it, they shouldn't go to war any more," just as if waging war were something extraordinary. Let the weak, timid and doubting consciences then be advised: If the exercise of power and the sword, as I have shown, is a service to God, then everything must be a service to God which power needs to wield the sword. And therefore the subjects are obliged to follow and stake their lives and goods. And in such a war it is Christian and a work of love amid the enemy to slaughter, rob, burn, and do everything which can cause damage, as is the way in wars. All a man needs is to beware of sin.

MAN'S VOICE   And if my lord is in the wrong?

LUTHER   When you do not know or cannot learn whether your lord is in the wrong, then you should not weaken your obedience, but put the best trust in your lord. Then you are sure and once again act rightly before God. For whoever fights with a good, rightly instructed conscience can also fight rightly. Everything succeeds better, and it is all the more fitting for victory, which too God gives. The heathen, who knew nothing of God and the fear of God, were of the opinion it was they themselves who waged war. But when the sword is appointed by God, it is proof enough that war and massacre and the things that war brings with it have been appointed by God. What is war other than the punishment of wrong and evil? Why is war waged but to have peace and obedience?

MAN'S VOICE   Why must we fight? We Christians ought to love our neighbor.

LUTHER   Consider for yourself—if we were to concede this point, that the waging of war itself is wrong, then we must concede all the other points and allow them to be wrong. If one work of the sword is good and right, then they are all good and right. A sword's a sword, not a tuft of feathers. Now it's true, it does not look as if massacre and robbery were a work of love. So some may think in their simplicity that it is not a Christian work and is not fitting for a Christian to do. But in truth it is a work of love. When I see how it slaughters the wicked and causes such great misery, then it seems utterly unchristian work and in every respect the opposite of Christian love. But when I see how it protects the righteous, maintains honor and peace, then it appears how precious and godly a work it is. That is why God so highly honors the sword which he calls his order. He does not want men to say or to think that it was invented or instituted by men. For the hand which wields this sword in slaughter is no longer the hand of men but the hand of God, and no longer is it the man who hangs, breaks on the wheel, beheads, and wages war, but God. They are all His works. And just as a good man of his trade can sell his skill to anyone who wants it, so it is too with a sol- dier. Because he has got his skill from God to do war service, let him serve with his skill whoever requires it and take his wages for his labor. A laborer is worthy of his hire. But what am I to think of those comrades who turn to their amours before a battle? I must say, if I had not heard from two trustworthy men that such things happen, I should never have believed that human hearts in so serious a cause could be so forgetful and frivolous.

Therefore we should thus warn them: Dear brethren, we are gathered here in the service of our lord in duty and obedience toward him. True, we are just as much poor sinners as our enemies, but yet we know that our lord is in the right, or at least we know nothing different, and so we are sure and certain that we with this service and obedience serve God Himself. So let every man be courageous and undaunted, let him not think otherwise than that his fist is God's fist, his spear God's spear. If God give us the victory, then honor and praise belong not to us but to Him. The plunder, however, and the wages we will take as something bestowed on us by His divine goodness and grace and thank Him for it from our hearts. Put yourself in God's hands and have at them with joy. If you want to say the creed and an Our Father to it, you may do so. And then draw and strike home in God's name. For Christian faith is no joke and no small thing, but can do anything. It will certainly bring some to God. The others who despise this message of salvation which serves their blessedness have their judge to whom they must answer. We are excused and have done our part. A soldier, you see, must have the good conscience that it is his bounden duty so to do, for he must be sure that he serves God in it and must be able to say "Here strikes, pierces, slaughters not my own self but God and my prince, whose servant my hand and body now are." So now as regards war there is no doubt that it is all something justified and godly. And the grace and peace of Christ be upon you.

PLATFORM LEFT

(MÜNZER *is standing on the steps. A big crowd in front of the platform.*)

MÜNZER   Dear brothers, let us widen the hole through which all the world may see and understand who our great lords are. They hide behind their profiteering commerce, clustering to one another like toads.

MAN'S VOICE   Nobody knows where to turn with all this slave-driving, profit, and interest.

MÜNZER   The ruin of the world gets longer, the broader and wider it gets. We neither will nor can see that such things are the doing of God's faith, and when we tell them they are not, they show their fangs and say "I want to start a rebellion." Oh, my good lords, be not so bold with your mad faith as to consign all others —yourselves of course excepted—to the Devil as you are always wont to do.

MAN'S VOICE   There's a fine traffic again in sending people to the Devil.

MÜNZER   With their snap judgments they make heretics of anyone who says a word against them. They write, Spirit here, Spirit there, and try with their assaults day and night how they may destroy those of us who try to say a word about the Spirit. I have said that the people have the power, that the princes are not masters but servants of the power. They are not to do as they please, they are to do right. If that is rebellious, well then. It is the greatest atrocity upon earth that nobody will do anything to relieve the most miserable distress.

MAN'S VOICE   The great people do what they want.

MÜNZER   They themselves are the cause of usury, theft, and robbery. They take all creation for their property. The fish in the water, the birds in the air, the plants of the earth, all must belong to them. And over it they give out God's commandment among the poor and say "God has commanded, Thou shalt not steal." While they compel all men thus, and while they grind down peasants, artisans, laborers, and everything that lives, yet if one man touches the tiniest thing, they hang him.

MAN'S VOICE   The lords themselves act so as to make the poor man their enemy.

MÜNZER   They talk of rebellion but will not remove its cause. How can it turn to good in the long run? For merely saying this I am branded as rebellious. So be it, then. Then Doctor Luther says we should hold even the wildest lords in honor, we should in all things be obedient to these kind lords. Oh for heaven's sake, they have spent their lives in bestial guzzling and tippling, from their youth on educated to all that is finest, have never had a bad day in their lives, nor will or intend to have one. Will not abate one farthing of their rents and want to be our judges and protectors. Oh you poor humankind, you have become nothing but a chopping block, for the lords are not lords because of their kind words but because of the fear of the gallows.

MAN'S VOICE They are nothing but hangmen and beadles. That is all their trade.

MÜNZER Their government raves and rages, showing its true self in all manner of wantonness, and many there are who now begin, worse than ever before, to harry and oppress their folk. Yes, they threaten the whole of mankind and torture and kill not only their own folk but other nations' as well. They would like to condemn all humankind, so that they alone may be supreme and be feared beyond all others, worshiped and held in honor. It is a worship of men, because men fear their lords, and must disguise their feelings for the sake of their miserable livelihoods. For the laborers' sweat tastes sweet to them, sweet.

MAN'S VOICE It will turn to bitter gall for them.

MÜNZER Here no scruples or prevarication will help, the truth must out. It shall no longer go on as it has gone till now. The game is up, the nations are sick and tired of it, everything is changing. Men in all the world are enlightened, and the mighty with their insensate power will yet be overthrown. For it is a mighty great impudence to want to employ the old means of power after the whole world has so greatly changed. Therefore do not let yourselves be brought by kind words to an abject compassion, then your cause will surely prevail. We must remember the Spirit. We must know, and not merely believe at random. For a man must have understanding. Let them blaspheme about all those things which they will not recognize. If they are given friendly warning, they refuse to hear or to see anything. They call all who think differently enthusiasts and do not like to listen when the word *Spirit* is read or said. Yes, it seems to the world the most impossible thing that the nations should be free.

MAN'S VOICE Countless folk believe it is all only enthusiasm.

MÜNZER They cannot judge otherwise than that it is impossible to push the masters from their seat and to raise up the lowly. That they don't want to hear, so there has to be enthusiasm in everything. Oh, my good lords, stop it. Throw your make-up box to the Devil. All your swindling has been shown up. Do you feel the great spark which is about to spring into a great fire? Yes, you feel it, and I feel it too.

(MÜNZER *goes off with the jubilant crowd*)

PLATFORM RIGHT

(GEILER VON KAISERSBERG *leans languidly at a lectern and preaches with low-voiced refinement. In front of him, sitting on chairs,* FUGGER *and a few society ladies and gentlemen.*)

GEILER   The rich are the evil of the world. *(Applause)* These gentlemen who live on usury, cause famine and scarcity and sit on their full coffers. *(Applause)* They should be driven out like wolves, for they fear neither God nor man. *(Applause)* The country is full of the poor and the weak, beggars and cripples lie on the streets, and on a banquet they spend half a million. And at dice they will stake even a million. In the midst of increasing poverty they enjoy their growing wealth. Truly, I say unto you, in view of such crass differences of property it will come to a revolution one day. *(Loud applause)*

FUGGER   *(getting up and pressing* GEILER'S *hand)* Dear Geiler von Kaisersberg, you have given us, as so often, one of your masterly sermons. Sermons which get under the skin. I venture to say that we shall none of us lightly forget your words of warning. *(Applause.* GEILER *bows)*

FUGGER   I have had a simple pea soup warmed up.

GEILER   Pea soup? I thought a cold collation.

FUGGER   You preached plainness. We do our best.

(GEILER *and the other guests go off.* SCHWARZ *comes on to the platform and gives* FUGGER *a bloody, hacked-off hand)*

FUGGER   What's that?

SCHWARZ   A hand.

FUGGER   The things that people think of. *(He gives the hand back to* SCHWARZ, *who lays it on the account book)* Where's the owner?

SCHWARZ   Perhaps the other parts are still to come.

FUGGER   Let's hope they forget nothing. Otherwise how is the poor fellow to be put together again?

SCHWARZ   They'll end by sending us three more heads, and there we shall be.

FUGGER   Sender?

SCHWARZ   The Knights' Party. Sickingen has struck.

FUGGER   And the Princes' Party?

SCHWARZ   Has no money, as usual.

FUGGER   (*makes out a check and gives it to* SCHWARZ) That should be enough. But I must emphatically request that the Knights' Party be liquidated. Totally.

SCHWARZ   I'll give the message.

FUGGER   Not only Sickingen. All of them. So that we have the whole gang off our necks.

SCHWARZ   The princes are very conscientious in these matters. Then only the workers and peasants will be left.

FUGGER   It'll soon be their turn. Why have you put the hand on the accounts? (*He takes it up*) Bloodstains! When I won't even allow inkstains. (SCHWARZ *erases diligently*)

FUGGER   (*considering the hand*) How these people wage war. Disgusting. That's no proper style.

SCHWARZ   Won't come out. You'll have to put up with it, blood in the balance sheet.

FUGGER   Let's say they're in the red and write it off. (*He gives* SCHWARZ *the hand*)

SCHWARZ   (*calling*) Herr Geiler von Kaisersberg! (GEILER *appears in front of the platform.* SCHWARZ *throws the hand down to him*) The cold collation.

GEILER   (*is delighted and goes off singing with the hand*) Thoughts are free, thoughts are free!

TABLE LEFT FRONT

MÜNZER (*and a few companions, bearded and long-haired.*)

MÜNZER   All are equal. Everything is in common and is to be distributed to each man according to his need. All power is to be given to the people. Whoever resists shall have his property confiscated, for by their money they have hindered justice from the very beginning. The people in their simplicity have put trust in their masquerade of splendor, and their unceasing clamor about right and justice.

1ST COMRADE　They'll go on clamoring and the people will go on putting trust.

MÜNZER　Our cause is like the fine red wheat. When it's hidden in the earth it seems as if it would never sprout. But it will sprout. Those in authority will be cast down, their clamor will help them not at all. They have lorded it long enough and they will not be excused. I have spoken before many men. The common man in all places accepts the truth. The folk have had all too much patience. The people is not stupid, it is intelligent. It is a people that will dare it. It wants to do right and not to fear the mighty of this world.

2ND COMRADE　Everyone thinks only of himself.

MÜNZER　But why is that so? Why? We must bring workers, citizens and peasants together. It won't do singly. They must understand: Their hurt is the hurt of all of us. Their demands are our demands. There is no other way to help this humankind except by showing them with all seriousness, with persevering sobriety, the alienation of this world.

HUT　I shall found a new community. A few people who want to live together and who then join up with other groups like them. Marriage can stay but the children will be brought up communally. Everyone gets what he needs. Community of goods. A communal kitchen, school, hospital. We shall work communally and buy communally, and we shall refuse all war service. For all war is sinful.

MÜNZER　Hut, you're a dear good fellow, but now it's a matter of establishing the conditions.

HUT　I shall found a new community.

MÜNZER　When we have won through, you can organize yourselves as you want. Now we need cells in all towns and states.

3RD COMRADE　That's just about the limit of what the lords will permit.

MÜNZER　It's the time of testing. Are you fond only of your possessions? Are you in fear of your life? He who will be a stone of the

new house must venture his neck. I'll take on the mine-workers.
We need the masses. And you?

1ST COMRADE Franconia.

2ND COMRADE Swabia.

3RD COMRADE Württemberg.

HUT I want to found a new community.

PFEIFFER I can see us all hang first. And the masses will buy tickets
to attend the spectacle.

MÜNZER I have no doubts of the people.

(All go off)

PLATFORM LEFT

SPALATIN The list of the Knights' castles destroyed.

FREDERICK Fine.

SPALATIN *(reading aloud)* Felberg, belonged to William of Felberg,
burnt. Boxberg, belonged to Hans Melchior, burnt. Balbach,
belonged to Rudiger Sutzel, burnt. Aschhausen, belonged to
to Hans von Aschhausen, burnt. Walbach, belonged to Franz
Rud, burnt. Waltmanshofen, belonged to Kunz von Rosenberg,
burnt. Reussenberg, belonged to George von Thüngen, burnt.
Kriegelstein, belonged to Wolf von Gich, burnt. Oppenroth, be-
belonged to Sebastian von Sparneck, burnt.

FREDERICK How many pages?

SPALATIN Ten.

FREDERICK I'll take it to bed with me. It'll read me pleasantly to
sleep. (SPALATIN *gives him the list*) I'm going to adopt a new
title, Supreme Performer of All Good Works in My State. Does
that sound well?

SPALATIN It sounds convincing.

FREDERICK Then enter it in the books.

SPALATIN Speaking of good works—

FREDERICK Münzer again?

SPALATIN Yes. The affair is developing very fast.

FREDERICK A smart lad.

SPALATIN That depends on the point of view.

FREDERICK Yes. Two great men is rather too many for one country. Luther I like, I approve of him, but Münzer is a nuisance. Invite him one day to come and lay his position before us. Let's see if he'll still have the courage.

SPALATIN Do you want to hear him personally?

FREDERICK No, I have nothing to do with the matter. Not the least thing. You know that. Old people do not change their habits. Let my brother take it on. It's time he started to work himself into the government a bit. *(He gets up and looks at the list)* Schloss Absberg, oh look at that, I dined there once. In the year '98. Now it's gone. The way of the world, well well. *(He goes off. SPALATIN follows him)*

TABLE RIGHT FRONT

(LUTHER is elegantly dressed. A coat of dark cloth, the sleeves slashed with satin. His cloak is lined with fur and has a broad fur collar. On his head he wears a wide red cap. About his neck a heavy gold chain. On his fingers gold rings. He is standing in front of a crowd of peasants brandishing a letter)

LUTHER All rebels. All enthusiasts. I can see you all in hellfire, every one of you. Rabble. Don't think I have much time for you. We have more important things to do in Wittenberg. Where's your pastor hiding, the clever gentleman? You'd do better to throw him out.

KARLSTADT *(steps forward. He is wearing a dirty gray peasant's smock and an old felt hat)* Is it me you want?

LUTHER What's the meaning of this get-up? Mardi Gras?

KARLSTADT It's the dress of the poor, and they as we all know have Mardi Gras all the year round because they're so well off.

LUTHER Just your case. *(To the people)* You have written me a hostile letter.

PEASANT Hostile?

LUTHER You don't give me my title. I insist on being addressed with the proper title. Even princes and gentlefolk who are my enemies give me my title.

PEASANT It wasn't done on purpose, nor hostile in—

LUTHER Here is written: To the Christian teacher Martin Luther, our brother in Christ. If that isn't hostile. Without any title.

KARLSTADT We're all brothers here. We don't have differences of rank.

LUTHER How so?

KARLSTADT We're all equal.

LUTHER Who?

KARLSTADT The citizens of our town.

LUTHER And you? What are you?

KARLSTADT Yes, what am I? I should say a new layman.

LUTHER You? Professor and twice Doctor.

KARLSTADT Here we no longer say "Master Doctor, Master Professor."

LUTHER What do you say then?

KARLSTADT Brother, neighbor. It isn't all that important.

LUTHER And what does "Master Neighbor" do?

KARLSTADT He labors. I earn my bread by the labor of my hands, as it is so finely put.

LUTHER As a peasant?

KARLSTADT As a peasant. I don't want to live at the expense of the community. People like us have lived far too long at others' expense. I wish I could give the poor folk everything back.

LUTHER And so you're a laborer?

KARLSTADT Yes.

LUTHER The real thing, plow, hoe?

KARLSTADT Yes.

LUTHER Mardi Gras after all. A peasant's smock that speaks Hebrew. *(He laughs)*

KARLSTADT Of what use to the people is a scholarship which only serves to keep authority in power? What you and all the other professors proclaim is quite unimportant for these folk here. But for centuries it has earned the applause of the rulers. It is paid for, promoted, expands, and finally even calls itself science. Such a science we will gladly dispense with. We need a new education. A new human being.

LUTHER Just your case, if you make common cause with the rabble.

KARLSTADT Don't you think, Luther, that these blisters are more honorable to the hands than golden rings?

LUTHER *(sticking his hands in his pockets)* You know why I'm here?

KARLSTADT I can guess.

LUTHER Your sermons excite displeasure.

KARLSTADT   In the Prince or in you?

LUTHER   In the Prince and in me.

KARLSTADT   Am I having too much success?

LUTHER   You preach rebellion. The people are becoming turbulent.

KARLSTADT   Where do you see rebellion here? Show me.

LUTHER   When I say rebellion, then it is rebellion. Pack up your things and come with me.

KARLSTADT   Where to?

LUTHER   Back into the University and the monastery.

KARLSTADT   So that you can have me under your control?

LUTHER   Pack your things.

KARLSTADT   I'm the pastor here.

LUTHER   We can compel you.

KARLSTADT   According to the old ecclesiastical law you can. But so far as I know you yourself have proclaimed that every congregation can freely elect its own pastor.

LUTHER   You are relieved of your post. *(The crowd murmurs)*

KARLSTADT   The congregation, it seems, is of a different opinion.

LUTHER   *(roaring at the peasants)* You shut your mouths. I needed three years for the true faith. I fancy you'll need rather longer.

KARLSTADT   It is nowhere written that God has appointed only Dr. Luther to proclaim His word. And even the people are asking why it is only Dr. Luther who can interpret the Bible in its true sense.

LUTHER   You will submit to the censorship of the University or your writings will be forbidden.

KARLSTADT   You'd bring even the Apostles to the stake. Yes, not Christ himself could stand up to you.

LUTHER   Peasant professor.

KARLSTADT   Princes' professor.

LUTHER   I know you, little man.

KARLSTADT   And I know you.

LUTHER   You want to put on a big act, lording it around the place, craving honor and respect.

KARLSTADT   I see the one who puts on a big act and lords it around, who prides himself above everyone and craves high honors.

LUTHER   That time in Leipzig, too, you were just as arrogant and wanted to appear in disputation ahead of me.

KARLSTADT   I had to. You were not admitted till later. You know that perfectly well. So why do you lie? You must always and everywhere be speaking so as to increase your own reputation and arouse hatred against others. What else have you done today but stir up the people against me? Go on, keep on at me then, others will know how to judge between us.

LUTHER   Do you want to write against me?

KARLSTADT   Why not?

LUTHER   Go to it, then, go to it, out with it, preach, write, attack me. I'll even pay you. Here's a hundred for you. (*He throws a gold piece on the floor.* KARLSTADT *picks it up*)

KARLSTADT   Dear brothers, this piece of gold is the proof that I have the right to write against Dr. Luther. You are witnesses. Make it known everywhere.

LUTHER   Witnesses, witnesses. That's not necessary. We need no witnesses, old fellow, here among ourselves. Have you any beer? (*Two mugs are handed over*) Here, old boy, your health. (*They touch mugs and drink.* KARLSTADT *and the peasants go off.* LUTHER *goes left*)

TABLE LEFT FRONT

LUTHER   I demand that Karlstadt be expelled from the state, immediately.

SPALATIN   He wants to come to Wittenberg and justify himself.

LUTHER   He must be expelled. Immediately.

SPALATIN   The congregation has written to us. Now in the middle of winter. He has a small child, and his wife is pregnant. The people are on his side, it'll only cause disturbances.

LUTHER   I insist upon it, and I insist upon it. And Münzer must go too. Both must go. Otherwise I can answer for nothing any longer. Rebellion, murder, revolution.

SPALATIN   Let us take care of that.

LUTHER   You take care? All at once? That's nice. In a thousand years nobody has stood up for the lords as I have done. I am the first to have given the rulers a good conscience.

SPALATIN As they gratefully recognize.

LUTHER I could almost boast that since the time of the Apostles the secular power and authority has never been so clearly defined as it has been by me. Even my enemies must admit that. The wages I have earned in thanks for that are to have my doctrine decried and damned as rebellious and opposed authority.

SPALATIN A journalist's mistake.

LUTHER To which you have industriously contributed. The burlesque you put on there in Worms with me will never be forgiven you. There you sat like masks and idols around the Emperor, who understood nothing of these matters, and I had to do what pleased you, and then against all justice you put me under the ban of outlawry.

SPALATIN Only *pro forma*, you know that.

LUTHER *(roaring)* But the world does not! How do I come out of it? As a rebel, insurgent, revolutionary. But you will see. I am the block that God puts in the way. If I die He will lay about Him.

SPALATIN You exaggerate, as always.

LUTHER And supposing my life is of such worth in God's sight that, when I am not alive, you will no longer be sure of your lives and your ascendancy? Supposing my death were to be the misfortune of all of you?

SPALATIN Please don't get hysterical.

LUTHER *(tearing open his coat)* Kill me then, please, here I am, kill me, and never bring me back to life. (SPALATIN *looks around in a bored way.* LUTHER *buttons up his coat again*) Yes, I know, I am not destined to suffer from the tyrants of this world, while others will be murdered and burned. Instead, all the more, I have to fight with the Devil.

SPALATIN Now that really is your affair.

LUTHER Karlstadt must be removed. He falsifies the true doctrine.

SPALATIN Good then. Expulsion.

LUTHER And Münzer too.

SPALATIN *We* are already dealing with him.

LUTHER Thank God.

    (Both go off)

PLATFORM LEFT

(*On the platform—played by Frederick—*JOHN OF SAXONY, *Frederick's brother. Beside him* FEILITZSCH. SPALATIN *and* MÜNZER *in front of the platform*)

SPALATIN   The Prince's brother awaits you. (*They go onto the platform.* SPALATIN *stations himself beside* JOHN *and whispers something to him.* JOHN *nods.* SPALATIN *to* MÜNZER) Go ahead. Your sermon.

MÜNZER   You lords who call good bad and bad good, the times are dangerous and the days are evil. A reform is greatly needed. Let everyone resist it as he may. Now we are told there's no advice or help will serve our poor, suffering, ruined humanity. But what are we to do when the world is so miserably devastated? How are we poor worms to come to any reform when we hold the dignity of the great in such respect that even Christ in comparison with the great titles and names of this world appears like a painted mannikin. What we see before our eyes is vain hypocrisy which twists and winds itself over all the earth and seduces men with big talk. Yes, they can babble prettily about the faith, the lords of this world. They appear in great kindness and patience, and nothing on earth has a better form and mask than their hypocritical goodness. Therefore it is that every corner is full of hypocrites, not one among whom is so bold as to tell the real truth. Because, they say, let the truth of itself come to light. But man must have a serious courage for the truth and must know the honest faces from the false. It is clear as day that nothing, God help us, is held in such ill and scant respect as the Spirit. It is obvious that they have taken Spirit for their laughingstock and do so still. They have robbed the people of their voice and have put money in its stead as their Lord God to make the poor folk smack their lips. For they want to own the whole world, so that they may unfold their splendor and in the end even believe that only they are great. But these godless people have no right to live. Christ says "Whoso shall offend one of these little ones, it were better for him that a millstone were hanged about his neck and that he were drowned in the depth of the sea." Let who will say it, they are the words of Christ. Now if Christ may say "Whoso shall offend *one* of these little ones," what are we to say if he offend a whole people so. That is what these filthy scavengers do who pretend to be more benevolent than God and despoil the whole world.

(JOHN *stirs with a growl*)

Yes, then that pretended, hypocritical goodness turns to anger. Don't cheat us with feeble pretenses that the strength of God must do it, without the aid of the sword. We shall not let ourself be seduced or checked by pretended patience and goodness, for the stone that has been set rolling has grown big. It has grown big and mighty, and the poor folk see it much more clearly than you. Oh dear lords; what a fine smashing there'll be there among the old pots with an iron crowbar. Therefore, you most dear, most beloved rulers, learn your sentence. Your power will be taken from you, for the weeds must be rooted out in the time of harvest. Then will the fine red wheat get firm roots and come up properly.

(JOHN *jumps up angrily. A short pause, then he turns to* SPALATIN *and whispers something in his ear.* SPALATIN *nods.* JOHN, SPALATIN *and* FEILITZSCH *go off.* MÜNZER *stands alone on the platform. He goes off*)

TABLE RIGHT FRONT

(*Two* JOURNALISTS *are waiting. They note down* LUTHER'S *answers.* LUTHER *sits down at the table*)

LUTHER   Here is cattle and byre, said the Devil, and drove a fly up his mother's behind. *(He laughs)*

1ST JOURNALIST   Doctor, why are your writings so abusive?

LUTHER   One who in our times wants to write tranquil treatises will be quickly forgotten, and nobody will bother about him.

1ST JOURNALIST   Doctor, how do you know that you have been chosen?

LUTHER   I am sure that my words are not mine but Christ's words, so must my mouth too belong to Him whose words he speaks.

2ND JOURNALIST   That is your opinion.

LUTHER I shall accord nobody, not even an angel from heaven, the honor of judging my teaching. He who does not accept my teaching will not be blessed.

2ND JOURNALIST Are you sure, Doctor?

LUTHER In Worms I stood before Emperor and Diet and did not budge. I am the German prophet. All Germany follows me, only on the strength of my words.

1ST JOURNALIST What do you think of the princes?

LUTHER Our God is a great lord and master, that is why He must have such noble, high-born, wealthy hangmen and beadles and wants them to get from every man in full measure riches, honor, and respect. It pleases His divine will that we call his hangmen gracious lords, fall at their feet, and subject ourselves in all humility.

1ST JOURNALIST And your Prince?

LUTHER I am satisfied with him.

2ND JOURNALIST Are you satisfied with yourself too?

LUTHER In a thousand years there has been no bishop to whom God has given such great gifts as to me.

2ND JOURNALIST There are people who allege that you lie.

LUTHER If a true heart dissembles, that is no lie.

1ST JOURNALIST Doctor, we hear everywhere nowadays of laymen who want to take part in disputations.

LUTHER There can be no question of it. It remains with the ordered offices of the Church and the prophets. If they do not teach right, what has that to do with the public? That would be a fine state of affairs, if anyone could break into anyone's discourse. The prophets speak and the congregation listens.

2ND JOURNALIST Doctor, what do you think of Erasmus?

LUTHER Erasmus is the greatest enemy of Christ there has been for a thousand years. In all his writings he has had not the cross in view but a paltry peace.

1ST JOURNALIST And of Copernicus?

LUTHER The fool wants to turn the whole of astronomy upside down. But that's how it goes today; anyone who wants to be thought clever must create something of his own.

2ND JOURNALIST Doctor, what do you say to the Mahometans?

LUTHER A disgraceful, lying, horrible faith. I am disgusted that human beings can let themselves be talked by the Devil into accepting such infamies.

1ST JOURNALIST   Doctor, what do you think of Dr. Münzer?

LUTHER   Whoever has seen Münzer has seen the Devil.

2ND JOURNALIST   In Allstedt he has introduced the German mass.

LUTHER   Are we talking about me or about Münzer?

2ND JOURNALIST   Why do you not introduce a German mass? Because it comes from Münzer?

LUTHER   We must first see whether God wants it.

1ST JOURNALIST   Is this God your Prince?

LUTHER   I leave that to God.

2ND JOURNALIST   What is your attitude to the Pope and cardinals?

LUTHER   Whoever has seen the Pope has seen the Devil. What he has is all stolen. That sodomite, that lecher with his hermaphrodites. I wish him plague, syphilis, leprosy and boils, and all other ills and diseases. Our princes should step in and take everything away from him. The whole pack should have their tongues torn out of their throats and nailed to the gallows.

1ST JOURNALIST   What do you think of the Jews?

LUTHER   Whoever has seen a Jew has seen the Devil. What they have is all stolen. The princes and the authorities sit by, snoring with their mouths wide open. The Jews should have nothing, and what they have should be ours.

2ND JOURNALIST   What should the authorities do?

LUTHER   First the synagogues should be set on fire and anything that won't burn stopped up with earth, so that no man may see a stone of them forever more. And that should be done for the honor of Christianity so that God may see we are Christians. Then their houses should be destroyed. Instead they may be put under a roof or in a stable, like gypsies, so that they may know they are prisoners and in penury. Their prayerbooks should be taken away from them and their rabbis forbidden on pain of death to teach. Then all their cash and jewels in silver and gold should be taken from them and put aside. The young, strong Jews and Jewesses should have flails, axes, mattocks, spades, and spindles put in their hands and be made to earn their bread by the sweat of their brow. But if we should fear that they may harm us when they serve us or work for us, let us be guided by our natural sense and settle our accounts with them; and once they have been dispossessed let them be driven out into the countryside.

1ST JOURNALIST   Doctor, what do you think of the Germans?

LUTHER   We Germans are Germans and remain Germans, that is swine and irrational beasts.

2ND JOURNALIST   And of the foreigners?

LUTHER   The Italians are artful. The French are lascivious, the Spaniards are savage. England makes fun of us.

1ST JOURNALIST   Doctor, what is your opinion about women?

LUTHER   They have two tits and a little hole between their legs. *(He laughs)* The wife should love, honor, and obey her husband. If the women wear themselves out with carrying and finally tire themselves to death, that does no harm, it's what they're there for. It's better to live healthy for a short while than unhealthy for a long while.

2ND JOURNALIST   And the students?

LUTHER   Undisciplined, immoral, disobedient.

2ND JOURNALIST   What does Heaven look like?

LUTHER   There will be a great light. Flowers, leaves, and grass, as lovely as emerald. Lapdogs with golden skins. It will be altogether very beautiful.

1ST JOURNALIST   What did Noah's ark look like?

LUTHER   Three hundred ells long, fifty broad, fifty high. Down below bears and lions and other wild beasts, the peaceable animals between decks with the feed, and up on top domestic animals and poultry. It was very dark inside. The story is miraculous and if it were not in the Bible not to be credited.

2ND JOURNALIST   When was the fall of man?

LUTHER   At two o'clock in the afternoon. God was silent till four or five.

2ND JOURNALIST   When will the Day of Judgment be?

LUTHER   Originally 1590. But now it will come sooner. I have reckoned it out.

1ST JOURNALIST   Are there devils?

LUTHER   We have in Wittenberg two thousand devils on the roofs; forty thousand are in the clouds. Prussia has many bad spirits. In Switzerland, not far from Lucerne, on a very high mountain,

there is a lake called Pilate's Tarn, the dwellings of the devils
are in that.
2ND JOURNALIST   You have to wrestle with the Devil a lot?
LUTHER   I know Satan well.
1ST JOURNALIST   Doctor, we thank you for the interview.

(*The* JOURNALISTS *go off*)

PLATFORM LEFT

(*A* CLERK, *two of* MÜNZER'S COMRADES, *and* MÜNZER,
whose hands have been tied behind his back. SPALATIN *comes
onto the platform.*)

SPALATIN   The letter. (THE CLERK *gives him a letter.* SPALATIN
strikes MÜNZER *in the face with it*) So that you know that a
prince is a prince. What's written here?
MÜNZER   To the Superintendent in Saxony.
SPALATIN   A prince (*Boxes his ears*) is a prince (*Boxes his ears*).
What's written here?
MÜNZER   To the Superintendent in Saxony.
SPALATIN   A prince (*Boxing his ears*) is a prince (*Boxing his ears*).
What's written here?
MÜNZER   To the Superintendent in Saxony.
SPALATIN   Then eat it. (*He sticks the paper in* MÜNZER'S *mouth.*
MÜNZER *swallows it*) Do you know the man?
1ST COMRADE   Never seen him before.
SPALATIN   And you?
2ND COMRADE   Yes, I know him, it's a cobbler from the Langen-
gasse.
SPALATIN   A cobbler?
2ND COMRADE   Yes.
SPALATIN   And you don't know him at all?
1ST COMRADE   When I take a longer look, he does seem a bit
familiar. I once had some business with a fellow from Osterode,
a certain Albert, he was a ropemaker.
2ND COMRADE   No no, this is a cobbler, I know.
1ST COMRADE   Oh, I mean the brother.
2ND COMRADE   What brother?

1ST COMRADE The ropemaker's brother.
2ND COMRADE I don't know him.
1ST COMRADE But he looked like him.
2ND COMRADE Like the ropemaker?
1ST COMRADE Like him there.
2ND COMRADE But that's the cobbler.
1ST COMRADE But actually there wasn't any likeness between them.
2ND COMRADE How should there be?
1ST COMRADE It was the brother.
2ND COMRADE That one hasn't got a brother.
1ST COMRADE Then it can't be he.
2ND COMRADE Well then, it isn't he.
CLERK Who?
1ST COMRADE ⎱ The cobbler.
                   (together)
2ND COMRADE ⎰ The ropemaker.
SPALATIN Our gracious Prince has a taste for comedies. Especially when they end with beheading. For conspiracy carries the death penalty.
1ST COMRADE Quite right too. Where would it get us otherwise? Our gracious lords wouldn't be safe in their beds any more.
2ND COMRADE The death penalty there must be. Mercy's no use. Only makes folk hard of heart.
SPALATIN Fine. Then you'll be beheaded as conspirators. We have here a membership list of your band.
2ND COMRADE I'm only in the church choir.
SPALATIN Here's your name.
2ND COMRADE I can only read music.
SPALATIN And here's your name.
1ST COMRADE There was a collection there once. Perhaps it's that?
2ND COMRADE That's right. I gave half a florin. The list of alms-givers.
SPALATIN *(to* MÜNZER*)* A nice pair, hm?
MÜNZER Yes, honest folk.
SPALATIN For a week he's been repairing the church roof.
MÜNZER Oh, that's who they are.

SPALATIN   He had a scrap of your writing in his pocket. The last shall be first.

MÜNZER   Yes, it was the text for one of my sermons. I must have dropped it.

1ST COMRADE   It was lying in the churchyard.

SPALATIN   And so you wanted to give it back to Münzer?

1ST COMRADE   I don't know him.

SPALATIN   (to MÜNZER) But you know him. He's in the church choir.

MÜNZER   The sexton looks after that. I am unmusical.

SPALATIN   And these names here you don't know either?

MÜNZER   No.

SPALATIN   And these fellows you don't know at all?

MÜNZER   No.

SPALATIN   We have witnesses.

MÜNZER   It's a big town. A greeting here, a greeting there, a friendly word from the other fellow. The way it is.

SPALATIN   (taking a new sheet) On the fourth you were sitting in the Golden Ox.

2ND COMRADE   Yes, so I was. I gave him my shoes.

SPALATIN   Gave Münzer?

2ND COMRADE   The cobbler.

SPALATIN   That's Münzer, you blockhead.

2ND COMRADE   Him?

SPALATIN   And you were sitting with him.

2ND COMRADE   Never. Do you think Münzer mends my shoes?

SPALATIN   Exactly. So what did you discuss?

2ND COMRADE   I gave him the shoes.

SPALATIN   Gave Münzer?

2ND COMRADE   The cobbler.

SPALATIN   But that is Münzer.

2ND COMRADE   He's lying, then.

SPALATIN   And what did you discuss with him on the sixth?

2ND COMRADE   I fetched the shoes. But that must be in the report there. Otherwise it isn't accurate.

SPALATIN   And on the ninth?

2ND COMRADE   My wife's shoes.

SPALATIN   And each time in the inn?

2ND COMRADE He's a tippler.

1ST COMRADE Just like the ropemaker.

SPALATIN (*roaring*) Throw the fellows out!

(*The* CLERK *pushes the two* COMRADES *off the platform*)

SPALATIN We'll get you yet. (*Goes off*)

CLERK (*untying the fetters on* MÜNZER'S *hands. In a low voice*) You're all under observation. They'll nab you all at your next meeting. At the south gate tonight there'll be a rope ladder. It'd be better for you to make yourself scarce before worse happens.

MÜNZER Thank you. Tell the others I'm going to Mühlhausen. There's something doing there.

(*Both go off*)

TABLE RIGHT FRONT

(LUTHER *is sitting with a beer mug in front of him, composing.*)

LUTHER (*singing*)
> An anthem new to God we'll raise
> God's might be in our voices

(MELANCHTHON *enters, with a bundle of papers under his arm*) Have you heard the news? I now have two martyrs. In Brussels they've burned two young lads. I have composed a little song about it.

MELANCHTHON Jolly.

LUTHER (*singing*)
> The great mistake these two did make
> In God alone they trusted—

I need something more.

MELANCHTHON
> Man lies and cheats his life away
> In him can not be trusted

LUTHER (*nods in agreement and sings*) Therefore the fire must burn them— That's good. (*He tries out various settings*) Must burn them, must burn them, must burn them, must burn them.

MELANCHTHON (*throwing down the papers in front of him*) From the court.

LUTHER   What a face you make.

MELANCHTHON   Everywhere church property is being confiscated. Here. A whole bishopric.

LUTHER   I know.

MELANCHTHON   All they're after is the cash. Nobody cares a damn about religion.

LUTHER   Yes.

MELANCHTHON   The princes only want the supremacy. Under cover of the gospel.

LUTHER   Yes.

MELANCHTHON   And the cover is knitted for them by us.

LUTHER   Yes.

MELANCHTHON   Yes. Yes. And meanwhile one monastery after another disappears.

LUTHER   Our task is to turn men's hearts away from it all. Once that happens, let the princes do as they like with it. It's all one to me. Let them pocket it. It all belongs to the Devil.

MELANCHTHON   To the princes.

LUTHER   Let things happen as they will. They will happen as they will. Why should we wear ourselves out? Let nobody suppose he can change the world. Would you like a beer?

MELANCHTHON   No.

LUTHER   You must sin more, Melanchthon. Only a hearty sinner can be forgiven by God. I eat like a Bohemian and drink like a German, thanks be to God. *(He sings)*

> Two great fires they kindled there
> The boys they brought in fetters

I should prefer that all my books had perished. But I have left it all to God. What is true, will have force.

MELANCHTHON   What the Prince enforces will have force.

LUTHER   As long as they can, they use us, afterward they grind our faces into the dust. Everything's gotten worse. Under the Pope folk were gentler. Now one oppresses the other, and all the princes care about are kitchen, cellar, and bedroom. If I could I should have them all back in the old church in three weeks. I am the mainstay of the Pope in Germany. They won't see until I'm dead what a boon I was to them. Others will not be so moderate as I.

MELANCHTHON   Just don't let the Prince hear you say that.

LUTHER If I had known what I know now I should never have let
myself be driven into it. Never. Ten horses wouldn't have dragged
me in. Verily I should have held my peace. But God dazzled my
eyes. If I could begin again I should do it differently. I'm a
simpleton sheep.

MELANCHTHON Why then do you go on preaching?

LUTHER So that they may say they have heard Luther.

MELANCHTHON I need your signature.

LUTHER Certainly it is a fine consolation to wear oneself out in
God's service. But there must be a measure in all things. *(He signs)*

MELANCHTHON I am worried. Deeply worried.

LUTHER And I get annoyed at your pitiful and superfluous worries.
You have fears for the whole of mankind. You worry about peace
and posterity. It is not our business to foresee coming wars. Our
business is to have simple faith and to confess it. Peace according
to our small understanding may have its value, as much as it
please. The giver of peace and the ruler of war is of more consequence than all peace. That is why I can look on at the course of
events in all tranquility. Our cause is just and true and the cause
of Christ. If we fall, Christ falls too. Another beer.

(*A* WAITRESS *brings a new mug of beer*)

MELANCHTHON I am unfortunately not on such good terms with
the Lord.

LUTHER You are tormented by your philosophy, nothing else. You
want to govern by reason. I admit you're well up in philosophy
but I'll have to chop philosophy's head off again one of these
days.

MELANCHTHON I'm a scientist, not a theologian.

LUTHER If science wants not to serve Christ but to trample on Him,
then it were better science should go under than religion.

MELANCHTHON Amen.

LUTHER For reason, it follows that there is no God at all.

MELANCHTHON Then we'll have to get rid of God.

LUTHER No, of reason. Reason is the greatest enemy of faith. It is
the Devil's greatest whore. It must be trampled underfoot and
destroyed with all its wisdom. Either the Word of God or the
voice of reason. We cannot listen to both, we must decide.

MELANCHTHON Then I choose reason.

LUTHER   For reason no religion is so foolish and so preposterous as the Christian. All the articles of faith in the light of reason are pure silliness. What is more impossible than that Christ in His Supper gives us His Body and Blood to eat or that the dead will be resurrected on the Last Day or that Christ, the Son of God, was conceived by the Virgin Mary, born of Her womb, became man, and died a shameful death on the cross. Or those stories with Jonah and the whale, the Garden of Eden and the serpent, Joshua and the sun. I could laugh at them. But it stands in the Bible, therefore we must believe it.

MELANCHTHON   I can believe no longer.

LUTHER   Well, thank God, it happens to others too. I thought I was the only one.

MELANCHTHON   What other purpose can Christianity have than to pacify souls and give them a pointer for their actions? The rest: hairsplitting of the schools, wrangling of the sects.

LUTHER   Why should we need a God only for this life? They enjoy life best who have no God. Now I cannot believe in the man Christ, and before I could believe in all sorts of rubbish. But we must not have such thoughts. God has forbidden them. We must shut our eyes and believe. We must have faith, faith, faith. Nothing to be done about it.

MELANCHTHON   I shall give notice.

LUTHER   Do you want to go away?

MELANCHTHON   I should like to do scientific work again. I'm dead sick of theological squabbling.

LUTHER   You are sent by God, you will stay.

MELANCHTHON   I am appointed by the Prince.

LUTHER   God appointed you here to help me.

MELANCHTHON   Would you like to see my letter of appointment?

LUTHER   Men's work. You're a work-tool of God.

MELANCHTHON   I am a professor paid by the Prince.

LUTHER   I'll back up the Prince and he'll forbid you to leave the country.

MELANCHTHON   Banishment or arrest. That is all your wisdom.

LUTHER   I am the prophet of Germania. So long as I live Germany shall have no distress. But when I am dead, then pray.

MELANCHTHON   *(getting up)* You're drunk. *(Goes off)*

LUTHER   Yes, so I am. *(He roars after the departing MELANCH-*

THON) Yes, so I am! *(He sings)*
>
> There is no lie they will not tell
> To sanctify the killing,
> With music loud and false as hell
> The voice of conscience stilling.

(With rapid speech)
>
> He that has begun it
> Will likely have to end it.

(He lays his head on his arms)

PLATFORM RIGHT

(On the platform MÜNZER *and* PFEIFFER. *In front of the platform* CITIZENS)

MÜNZER   Citizens of Mühlhausen, everywhere it is said that nobody follows my teaching because it is rebellious. Anyone who wants to have a clear judgment in this matter must indeed have no liking for rebellion, but he must also be no enemy of righteous indignation. He should use his reason, otherwise he will either too much hate or too dearly love my teaching. Neither of these do I want. We need a new council and a new court of justice. For the people must take part in the giving of justice. And when authority wants to distort judgment, then you must reject it. I know that you are afraid to pass a resolution. I will help you. Make a list of all the ill-usages, transgressions, crimes, injuries, and injustices of your lords and masters. Write them down so that everyone may see what sort of folk they are and what they have done to us. It will be an endless list. You will discover a hundred crimes of your authorities. Write them down. Let the list be printed. Lay it before all the world, for with that you can justify yourself to all the world. Whoever sees this list will not be able to find fault with you. It will be said that you have condoned too much and waited much too long and other cities and states will follow you. For the antagonisms have become great. It must have an end. How much longer will you feed on hope? There's little hope in your superiors. Their power is coming to an end. It will be given to the people, and then they will have to do right and justice such as they have never even dreamed of.

PFEIFFER   Who is in favor of the election of a new town council?

(The majority of the CITIZENS *hold up their hands)*

Good. Tomorrow there will be an election. Every precinct puts up a candidate. The new councilors will be paid by us. We shall expropriate the Church. We shall elect a new court of justice. No citizen may be arrested without cause. All taxes and Church levies will be reviewed, as will all debts and interest payments. The poor will be fed at the expense of the community. We can govern ourselves. Mühlhausen is a democracy.

(The CITIZENS *cheer)*

A CITIZEN   *(calling)* Münzer.
MÜNZER   What is it?
CITIZEN   Can we have another vote?
MÜNZER   The election is tomorrow.
CITIZEN   But we should so like to.
MÜNZER   Why?
CITIZEN   Just for the hell of it. It's fun.
MÜNZER   Well then, who's in favor? *(All raise their hand)*
Who's against? *(All raise their hand)*
Abstentions? *(All raise their hand)*
Passed. *(Laughter)*
(To PFEIFFER) I'm going to South Germany and into Switzerland. The peasants are waking up.

(Both go off. The CITIZENS *go left)*

PLATFORM LEFT

(In front of the platform PEASANTS *gather. They hold the Bible over their heads)*

SPEAKING CHORUSES
When Adam delved and Eve span
Who was then the gentleman?
1ST PEASANT   *(mounting the platform)* All men are equal. We want to be free men, we are not animals. We want a new order. We want to govern ourselves and have a say in our affairs. We want to elect new courts of justice. We want justice to apply to everyone. We demand a universal and free popular vote.

WORKMAN (*jumping onto the platform*) Brothers. I work in a mine. Fugger owns the mine. I produce ore. Fugger owns the ore. My brother works in a smelting plant. My brother processes the ore. Fugger sells the ore. Look what I possess and what my brother possesses. Look what Fugger possesses. Is that right? Is that in order?

MAN'S VOICE Take over the mines.

2ND PEASANT! (*jumping onto the platform*) We peasants slave all the year round, day in, day out, so that a few lords may lead the life appropriate to their station. What does "appropriate to their station" mean? How so are there different stations of men? Aren't we all human beings? Thousands of us work so that one man may live on it. Appropriate to their stations. In a palace. Why do they need palaces? Can't they live in ordinary houses like us?

MAN'S VOICE And why can't we move into the town occasionally and be citizens for a while?

1ST PEASANT Dear brothers, you've elected me your captain. Discipline. No ill-considered actions. We will demonstrate for our rights. We demand immediate negotiations. If the negotiations are agreed to, we'll go home again.

3RD PEASANT (*jumping onto the platform*) A dozen times we've negotiated with the lords. The negotiations have cost us four hundred thousand. And always, when we believed everything was at last clear, that swine rode away again and said everything was to stay as it was. Now he has raised the taxes twentyfold. Again we have negotiated for five days. Result: he threatens to send for the soldiers into the state.

1ST PEASANT Dear brothers, we have informed the lords in an orderly fashion of our league, with the express assurance that we don't want to use violence. We don't want bloodshed. We are peaceable folk. We will give our lords brotherly warning and a friendly invitation to join us. We don't want to offend anyone. Whoever joins us shall keep his palaces and estates. Whoever has rightfully acquired something may also keep it. A court of arbitration shall decide between us and the lords. We will appoint Luther and Melanchthon, those are the right people. They have a heart for the peasants. Until then everybody is to be obedient to the existing authorities, as is proper. Every act of violence against the authorities is strictly forbidden. Whoever contravenes this will be punished. The peace will be kept in the land unconditionally. Every man's property will be protected. Justice and the courts will function as hitherto and be respected by us. No man is to be deprived of his rights. The estates of the noble and ecclesiastical lords are to be especially protected. Arbitrary plundering or plotting of rebellion will be punished with death. The captains will take energetic measures. Interest and debts will continue to be paid. (*The* PEASANTS *murmur*) Yes, yes, do you want it to be said later "They didn't pay their debts, They're dishonest folk"? The taxes will be put on deposit until we have agreed with the lords on their future use. And let nobody venture to lay hands on Church property. Nothing may be taken away or sold. Exact accounts will be kept. Hans will now read out the army codes.

HANS Every village details four groups, who each serve eight days in turn at village expense. Officers and counselors remain with the Troop and will be paid to do so. To cover costs, a tax will be imposed. Every man has to pay two farthings. God's word will be preached to the Troop twice a day.

MAN'S VOICE Once would do.

HANS Blaspheming, cursing, drinking, gaming, and immorality are forbidden. Prostitutes will not be tolerated.

MAN'S VOICE There's not a monastery would be so strict.

HANS The Troop will be divided into Groups of five hundred men each. Every Group will elect its own captain, ensign, corporal, purser, provost, quartermaster, master of ordnance, baggagemaster, commissary of stores, foragemaster, chief cashier, and sergeant-major.

MAN'S VOICE Then we really have something to do.

HANS At the head stands the senior field captain, as his deputies the lieutenant and the mayor. At his side the peasant counselor. Without the agreement of the peasant counselor no letter may be sent or received. For the office we shall need clerks.

A PEASANT Long live the revolution! Death to the princes!

1ST PEASANT That man will be arrested at once. (*All go off*)

TABLE RIGHT FRONT

(MÜNZER *enters*)

LUTHER God be with you.

MÜNZER God be with you. *(He sits down)* It is time, Luther. The time of harvest is upon us. Don't flatter your prince. We cannot do it any other way.

LUTHER The Devil. He wants to kill me. With cunning and force he hasn't managed it yet, but now he will dare it. The Devil is doing it all only on my account, getting the world into such a tangle. I am the reason. He wants to get rid of me. He often wanted to kill me before. He caused prophecies to be uttered which pointed to me. Oh, I know him.

MÜNZER The people want to be free.

LUTHER The Devil and his preacher.

MÜNZER I have done nothing else but tell the people that men should not so miserably victimize one another in this slaughter-house. And if our great lords will not permit that, then their power must be taken away from them. I shall not seal my lips. Conditions must be exposed. Folk are hungry. They want to eat.

LUTHER Go ahead then, with God's help I'll prepare myself for death and wait for my new lords, the murderers and robbers, to tell me that they mean no harm to anyone.

MÜNZER The lords may keep their lives and as much of their estates as they need.

LUTHER Let who will believe that, I won't. He who dares so great an injustice as to deprive authority of its power will take everything away from it. The wise man says *Cibus, onus, et virga asino.* Fodder, loads, and the cudgel for the ass. Oatstraw is the stuffing for peasants. If they won't hear that they must hear the bullets, and serve them right. We should pray for them to obey, and if they don't there can be no mercy. Let the bullets rain down on them.

MÜNZER Yes, you've become a confirmed soul-saver, with martyrs, a little hymn, and all the trimmings. A convenient faith for the rich, and for the poor the honeysweet Christ.

LUTHER   Christ has revealed Himself to me. I know the true faith.

MÜNZER   Yes yes.

LUTHER   At the risk of my life I had to dare it. I went in fear of bloodshed.

MÜNZER   Yes, I know you insist on those great persecutions you have to suffer. So that nobody notices how you yourself persecute the truth. Altogether I wonder you've been able to hold out so long against these atrocious persecutions—with all that good beer. Who do you expect to deceive? You had that good time at Leipzig, garlanded you rode out of the city gates, and drank good wine. And in Augsburg you had your counselors.

LUTHER   In Worms I stood before Emperor and Diet.

MÜNZER   The way you boast we should all be fainting at the thought of your fantastic foolhardiness in standing before the Diet at Worms. Give thanks to the German nobility whose lips you so liberally smeared with the honey of your sermons. You promised them monasteries and benefices. If you had wavered at Worms you'd have sooner had a knife in your back than be set free, as everybody knows. And then you let yourself be taken prisoner and put up a show of great unwillingness. Anyone who didn't know what a rogue you are might swear to God you were a pious man. And now, when the truth will out, you sit and scold the little men, not the great ones. Why do you crawl to the princes? So as to preserve your great name? Why do you call them serene highnesses? Why do you call them highborn when they trample Christ underfoot?

LUTHER   Whether they are Christians is unsure. That they are princes is sure. Therefore we should let the unsure go hang and stake our game on what is sure.

MÜNZER   A sure game, with God to clean up after.

LUTHER   The frogs must have their stork, to tear off their heads. Everything belongs by right to the Prince. The Prince is an excellent man, I have no doubts about him. We sit under his protection here as in a rose garden. But apart from him there's nobody I don't find suspect. If the Prince were not watching over us, we should have been not only starved out but murdered by the peasants, by the nobility, and by the citizens. And with it all there are no poor folk any more as once there were; workers are not to be had. I don't understand it. The people haven't the sense of an ass, to acknowledge the master who beats it.

MÜNZER The rulers are not to be judged by anyone, you say, and to keep the peasants quiet you write that the princes will be punished by God's word. All will be put right on the Day of Judgment. If this instruction were only passed on to the courts, the peasants too might for once get some benefit. They could postpone it to the Day of Judgment when they were sentenced.

LUTHER Pain pain, cross cross is the Christian's lot.

MÜNZER Provided the Christian is a peasant and not a lord. Do you suppose the whole country doesn't know what kind of a watch and ward they keep?

LUTHER If it doesn't suit the peasants they can emigrate.

MÜNZER How would it be if the Prince were to emigrate?

LUTHER Stop your sinning. The Swiss began that way and now they're worse off than before. Neither fear nor discipline.

MÜNZER Folk are to suffer and not defend themselves. That would be a great thing for the lords. Who made them lords of the people?

LUTHER God.

MÜNZER The light must be darkness, and the darkness of self-interest must be the light. That's what they preach to the people. The people don't know they're a hundred times, a thousand times worse off than before. From now on they'll be swindled with a new logic. With the word of God.

LUTHER *Mundus vult decipi.* The world wants to be deceived.

MÜNZER And so the people believe now that the authorities too were appointed by God. They believe it a crime to defend themselves against authority.

LUTHER Yes. That's the way things are. You can grasp with your reason that two and five are seven, but if authority says that two and five are eight, you must believe it, against all knowledge.

MÜNZER Anyone who can't swindle with that logic must be weak in the head.

LUTHER It's good that people revile me as a hypocrite. I'm glad to hear it. It must and will happen as I have written. There's nothing to be done about it.

MÜNZER You and your false humility. The harm you've done with your fanatical double talk. Truly a blasphemous thing, to treat human beings with such impudent contempt. Are they never to be allowed to take charge of their own affairs?

LUTHER   For that you must produce a special command of God, confirmed by signs and wonders. If God changes anything, he always accompanies it with wonders. Where are your wonders?

MÜNZER   I work without trickery.

LUTHER   My God will prevent your God from performing wonders without the will of my God. Evil must not be resisted. Whoever takes your cloak, leave him your coat also.

MÜNZER   Already done. Most people are left with nothing but a shirt.

LUTHER   Then they should humbly pray for redress, and if they don't get it, they should patiently suffer it and thank God they can live in peace and have enough to eat.

MÜNZER   If there's any food to be had and the lords are not waging a war just at that moment.

LUTHER   Man is unfree, like a log, a stone, a pillar of salt.

MÜNZER   Yes, yes, the freedom of a Christian man. When a people pushes a few lords aside, it's rebellion and insurrection. When the lords batter a whole people to pieces, peace and order reign. One day you must explain this logic to me.

LUTHER   What you're doing is revolution.

MÜNZER   What you're doing is a *coup d'etat.*

LUTHER   It is the lesser evil. The mob needs a strict, harsh government. Nobody must suppose that the world can be ruled without bloodshed. The lords too have the tools of their trade and they are no wreaths of roses or love garlands. Who has ever seen anything more undisciplined than the peasants? The ass must have beatings and the mob must be ruled by force.

MÜNZER   Thou shalt not despise these little ones.

LUTHER   The people would become much too arrogant if great burdens were not put on them. (He takes a sheet of paper in his hand) Here, look what comes of it. The twelve articles of the peasants. They want to abolish taxes.

MÜNZER   Apparently you can't read. It says here expressly that they want to pay them. They want to pay the pastors with them, to feed the poor. to pay war dues. They want to spend the tax money on that for which it is collected and not fill the lords' private coffers with it.

LUTHER   That is robbery, highway robbery. It all belongs to the authorities. They talk as if they were already masters in the land. Here. No more serfs. That's theft and against the gospel, that's everyone taking his body away from his master. In the Bible it is written "Abimelech has taken sheep and oxen, bondmen and bondmaids," those are all bodily owned goods, like the rest of the cattle. They could sell them as they wanted. It would be better if it were so today, how else are the folk to be compelled. Do you want to make all men equal? That's impossible. The world can only exist if men are unequal. Free and bond, masters and subjects.

MÜNZER   I believe you really can't read. Here is written they want to continue in obedience to authority. They only do not want to be serfs.

LUTHER   All these things are no concern of a Christian, and I don't ask about them. He must let anyone steal, take, oppress, guzzle, and rage. He is a martyr on earth. *(Takes another sheet of paper)* Here. Erfurt. Election of council. If the council isn't trusted why do they appoint one at all?

MÜNZER   The council must render account of its actions.

LUTHER   So that the council may be no council, and that the mob may rule.

MÜNZER   All power to the people.

LUTHER   To the mob.

MÜNZER   To the people.

LUTHER   I tell you, to the mob. Here. Usury to be abolished. Oh yes, perhaps the lender should pay interest in the bargain. I'd rather keep my money. Give another man money without interest? I'm not an infant. That lot are too well off. If I were lord of Erfurt, as a punishment for such unheard-of audacity, they'd have to suffer the opposite of their demands. It's turning things upside down. So that it's always authority which suffers damage, so that the council fears the people and is its slave, and the people is lord and master. That would make a fine city, I'm thinking. They should pray God that the princes do not step in and drive out their arrogance. God lives and reigns still. He will not abandon us.

MÜNZER *(roaring)* Listen, you village idiot—

LUTHER None of that, none of that. I won't listen. Give over. You'll achieve none of it.

MÜNZER In the Bible it says—

LUTHER If you thump the Bible against Christ, then we will force Christ home against the Bible.

MÜNZER The people will be free.

LUTHER *(roaring)* Where authority is not obeyed, everything the people are and have is forfeit. There you have rebellion and murder!

(MÜNZER *and* LUTHER *go off*)

PLATFORM LEFT AND TABLE LEFT FRONT

(*On the platform* ALBERT *and his* ADJUTANT. *In front of the platform three* PEASANTS.)

1ST PEASANT *(calling up to the platform)* God be with you, Master Prince, we are the revolutionaries.

ALBERT Oh, but that's nice of you to look in.

(*He comes down from the platform, his* ADJUTANT *following*)

2ND PEASANT *(kicking the* 1ST PEASANT) He is Elector.

3RD PEASANT(*kicking the* 1ST PEASANT) And Cardinal.

1ST PEASANT Where's the paper? Where's the paper? *(He reads)* Right honorable, well-born, noble, gracious, very learned, stalwart, prudent, wise, merciful lord and elector of—

ALBERT But please, my dear good friend. Why all the titles? Sound and smoke. Am I not right?

1ST PEASANT Well really, yes—

ALBERT There, you see.

1ST PEASANT Yes.

ALBERT What can I do for you?

2ND PEASANT Well, the matter's like this. We have assumed power.

ALBERT Yes, so I heard. Is it fun?

3RD PEASANT The responsibility!

ALBERT You're telling me!

1ST PEASANT Yes.

ALBERT Yes.

2ND PEASANT If Your Electoral Highness would just sign this here.

ALBERT Of course. Of course.

3RD PEASANT The twelve articles.

ALBERT Interesting. Twelve articles. Well well.

1ST PEASANT Do you know them?

ALBERT No.

1ST PEASANT Shall we read them out to you?

ALBERT Not necessary. Paper work.

2ND PEASANT In case an article should be unseemly, we beg you graciously to scrutinize it.

ALBERT No cause. *(He signs)*

1ST PEASANT Well, then. You're no longer a lord. Now you are our brother and a fellow human being like ourselves.

ALBERT Interesting.

1ST PEASANT Brother Albert, a hearty welcome. *(He shakes his hand and embraces him)* I am Brother Melchior, this is Brother Balthazar, this is Brother Caspar. *(They greet one another very warmly)*

ALBERT Yes, dear brothers, may I invite you? A little something to eat?

2ND PEASANT You do us honor.

ALBERT *(to his ADJUTANT)* Order a small buffet to be served. *(The ADJUTANT gives a sign to the rear, but stays near ALBERT)* Yes, let's sit down then. *(They sit down)* Come here, Brother—what was the name?

1ST PEASANT Melchior.

ALBERT Brother Melchior. Right. Correct.

2ND PEASANT Yes.

ALBERT Do you know this one; a bishop comes naked out of the confessional—

THE PEASANTS We know that one, we know that one. *(They laugh)*

ALBERT Yes.

1ST PEASANT Yes.

ALBERT   A little game?

3RD PEASANT   With pleasure.

ALBERT   *(taking up a dice box and banging it on the table)* Fourteen low. *(He hands on the dice box)* Yes, how is it to be now between us?

1ST PEASANT   You are now our brother, and we will defend your rights with body and soul.

ALBERT   Defend?

1ST PEASANT   Yes. You only have to command.

ALBERT   Oh I see— But expropriation?

2ND PEASANT   No, no, no question of it. No brother is to be deprived of anything. You keep your castles and all your property. *(He gives ALBERT the dice box)*

ALBERT   Pardon me. I can keep everything?

3RD PEASANT   And as compensation you get the Church estates.

ALBERT   *(the dice box falls out of his hand)* Pardon. I'm a bit confused. How was that? I get the Church estates?

1ST PEASANT   As compensation.

ALBERT   Compensation? What for?

1ST PEASANT   Because we now have the power.

ALBERT   Oh I see; yes, yes of course, I understand. Yes.

2ND PEASANT   You see, brother, the new order. Just let us handle it. We'll collect all dues for you. We'll make you richer than you've ever been.

ALBERT   Yes then— *(He bangs the dice box on the table)* 168 high. *(He hands on the dice box)* But if something were to be destroyed, you would have to pay me compensation.

1ST PEASANT   Goes without saying.

ALBERT   That'll cost a bit. New buildings are expensive these days. No doubt a great deal has been destroyed?

2ND PEASANT   Nothing.

ALBERT   Nothing? But surely here and there a castle, a monastery?

1ST PEASANT   No, no, nothing, nothing at all. It's all very strict with us. We mustn't touch a thing.

ALBERT   But that's a problem now. That's the purest pilgrimage you're making, then. I thought you'd be tearing everything down.

3RD PEASANT   Then we should have to replace it afterward.

ALBERT   Yes, that's just the reason. Cash. I'd already been counting on it. You know, here close by I have a few old shacks due for rebuilding. A hunting lodge, an old abbey. I've long been wanting to—you understand? I have plans there for a new building.

2ND PEASANT We have strict orders. We must not.

ALBERT But dear brothers, you won't let me down? In a revolution everything gets smashed to pieces. Everybody knows that. It's in every history book. Revolutionaries destroy everything. Well, what about it? (*The* PEASANTS *have scruples*) I'll pay every man a florin. . . . Well, let's say two florins.

3RD PEASANT Very good, then, for you, brother.

ALBERT Only it must happen quickly.

2ND PEASANT We'll detail a thousand men.

ALBERT But thoroughly. Not one stone left standing on another. A real destruction.

1ST PEASANT You can rely on us.

ALBERT (*banging the dice box on the table*) Chicago. I'm out.

ADJUTANT If I may be permitted to remark, I still have my ancestral castle.

ALBERT Ancestral castle? A crumbling rat's nest.

ADJUTANT Admittedly it is no longer habitable. But what does that signify? It is the ancestral seat. There are spiritual values to be considered. (*To the* PEASANTS) Couldn't you do something there too?

2ND PEASANT No no, that's impossible. An ancestral seat now as well. How are we to manage that?

ADJUTANT It's already fairly ruinous. It wouldn't take much labor.

1ST PEASANT Impossible.

ADJUTANT Just my luck. For a thousand years there hasn't been such a chance, and I have to miss the connection with the new age.

3RD PEASANT Pull it down yourself.

ADJUTANT Oh, that would be all right?

3RD PEASANT Of course that would be all right.

ADJUTANT Yes, I only mean, well, hm—well because of the spiritual values, well then the compensation—

ALBERT You are compelled—isn't it so, dear brothers, you said he should pull it down.

3RD PEASANT If it's uninhabitable.

ALBERT   An absolutely clear case. Falls under the compensation.

ADJUTANT   I'll just quickly tell the others.

ALBERT   Only I should hurry if I were you. It won't make a good impression when everything's over if you are all there still poking away at your castles.

ADJUTANT   *(going off in jubilation)* Compelled. Compelled.

1ST PEASANT   The parliament will be meeting very soon in Heilbronn, and everything will be settled there.

ALBERT   Parliament? What's that?

2ND PEASANT   Well, there's been an election, from every state a few people, and they're our delegates. Yes, and they are meeting in Heilbronn to consult about how things are to go on now in Germany. So that we have an order, a constitution, and so on. That's the parliament.

ALBERT   *(with a dismissive nod)* Politics.

3RD PEASANT   In England they have one already, they say.

ALBERT   England doesn't exist, at all. That's just a rumor.

ADJUTANT   *(entering and calling)* Your Electoral Highness!

ALBERT   Tear them down, tear them down.

ADJUTANT   Your Electoral Highness. *(Meaningfully)* The spices from Fugger.

ALBERT   Excuse me a moment. The menu. *(He gets up and goes over to his ADJUTANT. They whisper)*

2ND PEASANT   A nice gentleman. Speaks to the likes of us as to his own equals. As if he were a common man.

1ST PEASANT   He gave me his hand too.

3RD PEASANT   He even clapped me on the shoulder.

2ND PEASANT   It isn't the lords who are bad that way. That's only the stewards and officials. The lords know nothing of all that.

3RD PEASANT   And how well-educated he is. England doesn't exist at all.

ALBERT   *(coming back)* My brothers, I've just heard the food is on the table. Soup's on, plunge in your spoons.

(The PEASANTS go off laughing)

ADJUTANT   *(taking the document from the table)* And this?

ALBERT   Those, I think, are the nineteen Articles, or was it fifteen? I forget.

ADJUTANT You signed it.
ALBERT For the state archives. *(Both go off)*

PLATFORM RIGHT

(On the platform FUGGER *and* SCHWARZ, *who is busy with the mail. In front of the platform a throng of* PRINCES, *except for* FREDERICK *and* ALBERT)

SCHWARZ The people of Wels have written to Count von Mansfeld to ask if the rebels could please destroy our smelting works in Thuringia as well.
FUGGER Did they destroy them?
SCHWARZ No.
FUGGER You see, they'll never manage it all. All the places they're supposed to destroy. They'll need two years to carry out all their commissions.
SCHWARZ Our manager bribed them just in case.
FUGGER Waste of money. They won't destroy their own places of work.
SCHWARZ They've now summoned a parliament.
FUGGER Parliament? Anything to do with bookkeeping?
SCHWARZ No.
FUGGER What use is it, then?
SCHWARZ *(pointing to the* PRINCES) Shall I let them in? It's high time if we want to make a killing.
FUGGER You must catch the prices at their lowest level, then you can earn.
SCHWARZ Or lose everything. The workers are demanding expropriation and nationalization of mines.
FUGGER An astonishing thought. How could such an idea possibly occur to anyone? Monstrous. Positively inhuman. How much do the German mines bring in?
SCHWARZ Two hundred fifty million a year.
FUGGER That is an argument against the revolution. Let the gentlemen in.

(SCHWARZ *nods. The* PRINCES *storm onto the platform)*

1ST PRINCE My very dear Fugger—

FUGGER   Cross yourself first. This is a Christian house.

(*The* PRINCES *cross themselves*)

1ST PRINCE   My very dear Fugger. The peasants. All Germany is lost.

FUGGER   All Germany? You are lost.

2ND PRINCE   We're all in the same boat. If you won't pay, it's all up.

FUGGER   Apparently not. For you are rulers without subjects, whereas I am still a royal merchant with money. Or have I got the picture wrong?

3RD PRINCE   My very dear Fugger. For months now we've been holding off the peasants with negotiations. We've reached the point where we have no more concessions to make. And they're becoming distrustful.

4TH PRINCE   They smell a rat. You must pay now.

FUGGER   I must do nothing.

3RD PRINCE   It is not the right moment now for—

FUGGER   Oh yes it is. The very moment. Isn't that so, Schwarz?

SCHWARZ   Some of the gentlemen lately have been venturing to pull long faces over the monopolies.

PRINCES   Mistakes. Misrepresentations, distortions. Malicious slanders.

FUGGER   These are heretical opinions, gentlemen. Isn't that so, Schwarz?

SCHWARZ   (*positioning himself in front of the* PRINCES) Good kind Fugger is our watch and ward and without him we are nothing. —Well. I'm waiting.

PRINCES   (*in chorus*) Good kind Fugger is our watch and ward and without him we are nothing.

SCHWARZ   Once more.

PRINCES   Good kind Fugger is our watch and ward and without him we are nothing.

SCHWARZ   That's better. But not loud enough yet.

PRINCES   (*shouting*) Good kind Fugger is our watch and ward and without him we are nothing.

FUGGER   That's right. The common folk must hear it too. So that they mark, learn, and inwardly digest it. At ease!

1ST PRINCE   Money?

FUGGER   Securities. But don't come offering me your lands.

2ND PRINCE   Well, what else?

3RD PRINCE   We have nothing else left.

FUGGER   I'll take only gold and silver, at favorable prices, of course.

4TH PRINCE   Where from?

FUGGER   Take the chalices and crucifixes of the Church, melt them down and allege afterward it was the peasants who did it. Then you can even claim compensation from them as well.

(*Jubilation among the* PRINCES)

SCHWARZ   Stand forward. (*All the* PRINCES *rush forward*) One by one, you rogues! Country?

1ST PRINCE   Austria, Tyrol.

FUGGER   Ten million.

1ST PRINCE   And cannon.

FUGGER   Good.

2ND PRINCE   Württemberg, Swabia, Franconia, the Black Forest, Allgaeu, Lake Constance—

FUGGER   All South Germany.

2ND PRINCE   Yes.

FUGGER   Ten million.

2ND PRINCE   Hardly enough.

FUGGER   Have them plunder.

3RD PRINCE   Thuringia and Saxony, Münzer.

FUGGER   Münzer, a million and a half. (*To the other* PRINCES) The other gentlemen will be dealt with by my bookkeeper. (*To all the* PRINCES) But make a good job of it, gentlemen.

1ST PRINCE   We shall cut them down and slaughter them without mercy, burn down their houses and drive out their women and children. Better a ruined state than a lost one.

2ND PRINCE   And the prisoners we'll chop to pieces in the most delightful and well-mannered way. Before that just a little of the great and the small torture so that they don't feel neglected.

3RD PRINCE   Our fathers put a heavy yoke upon them but we shall make it heavier still. Our fathers chastized them with whips but we shall chastize them with scorpions.

FUGGER   A good government program. A genuine alternative.

Clear, decided, sober, realistic. How many will be taught this lesson?

3RD PRINCE   A hundred thousand. In for a penny, in for a pound.

FUGGER   Don't kill too many or you'll end by having to plow your own fields. *(Laughter)* And take good note for all time that *your* Germany was preserved by my money and not by the will of the people. Off with you. *(All* PRINCES *go off)*

SCHWARZ   I have here a rough balance of twenty-five million.

FUGGER   Against a hundred thousand dead peasants. That makes two hundred fifty per peasant. Works out cheap. Good business.

SCHWARZ   As always.

FUGGER   I want to earn money as long as I can. I have many enemies who say I am rich. I am rich by God's will. Do nobody ill. *(Both go off)*

PLATFORM LEFT

(HIPLER *and some* DEPUTIES *at a table. At the side a* CLERK.)

HIPLER   *(rising and ringing his bell)* I hereby open the first sitting of the first German Parliament. For the first time freely elected delegates of the people come together to take into their own hands the fate of Germany and to find a better and juster order for this country. I am convinced that the German people will never forget this day. It will be the beginning of a German democracy. I know that our enemies call us robbers and murderers, but the German nation—here I am quite sure—will never allow its ancestors, who under great privations fought for and won their right to self-determination and freedom and established a parliament, to be called beasts, plunderers, robbers, and incendiaries. On the contrary, I believe that every child will one day know the names of the deputies of this parliament and their political program as they will also know the twelve articles of the peasants. *(He sits down)* Point 1 of the order of business.

1ST DEPUTY   I have here yet another treaty.

2ND DEPUTY   That is not Point 1.

1ST DEPUTY   But it is important. What's the good of these treaties? Immunity, arbitration, obedience, and the peasants sign and go home.

HIPLER   But we have a foundation of law.

1ST DEPUTY   But all we ever do is make concessions. The treaties are much more favorable for the lords. The duties of the peasants are actually increased.

HIPLER   True. But we have a foundation of law. We do want at all costs to avoid violent disputes. So we must make concessions. But then we have a treaty. Do you understand?

1ST DEPUTY   No.

2ND DEPUTY   I propose Point 1 of the order of business.

HIPLER   Gentlemen, here we need no longer discuss the revolution. The German revolution has conquered. The people in all the important states hold the power. Most of the princes, the ordinary nobility, the cities, have joined us without resistance. Individual territories off the beaten track will no longer hold up the course of events. Here we have to discuss the construction of a new commonwealth. The deputies during the coming days have to report on the situation in the individual states, what anxieties they have, what can be changed, improved, where help can be given. We ought also to exchange programs and constitutions. The important thing is: We must return as quickly as possible to normal conditions. People must return to work. The troops can to a large extent be disbanded. A small police force should be enough to maintain order. Serfdom is to be abolished. The peasants, artisans, laborers, and citizens are freed from all Church dues. The Church estates are nationalized. The proceeds will be used to meet commonwealth expenses and to compensate the princes. This is generally the most important point, how the princes are to be incorporated in this commonwealth. For their loss of power they will of course be compensated. But they can continue to exercise certain functions.

2ND DEPUTY   Why shouldn't they remain as heads of state? We should be maintaining a good German tradition.

1ST DEPUTY   I am in favor of introducing new traditions.

2ND DEPUTY   You're a Münzer man.

HIPLER   (conciliatory) We all want democracy.

1ST DEPUTY   But do the princes want it?

HIPLER   The princes have signed the treaties.

1ST DEPUTY   They ought to surrender their power entirely. I propose that the new heads of state be elected, without consideration of birth, by the entire nation from among twelve men who will be put forward by the peasants. These new rulers too can be deposed if they make mistakes and have been warned three times by the state parliament.

3RD DEPUTY I propose a constitutional committee to settle these questions. They will include the position of the Emperor. He could without doubt remain as the nominal supreme head of state.

4TH DEPUTY How is the committee to be composed?

3RD DEPUTY We must give everybody a say. Let's say: twelve from the nobility, twelve from the cities, twelve from the people, and seven clergy.

1ST DEPUTY The Church has no place in government, not even advisory. The priests must keep their hands off all secular matters. They have enough to worry about with God.

CLERK Is that to go into the record?

HIPLER I also am in favor of separating Church and state. Especially at this time when we are faced with the Reformation business. Agreed? (All nod) Then first, please, the individual departments. I begin at once with foreign affairs. We must consider how we are to reach agreement with the foreign princes. Above all we must reckon with aggressions. Even the Emperor might come against us with troops. We must make preparations for this event.

2ND DEPUTY A standing army for the next few years will be indispensable.

HIPLER I propose we examine this more closely in the foreign affairs committee. Agriculture.

2ND DEPUTY Forests, lakes, and rivers are once more free and common property, except where they were rightfully acquired. For their administration executive decrees must be issued. Hunting rights, fishing rights, and so on. We are already engaged upon it.

HIPLER Good. Referred to committee. Industry.

1ST DEPUTY Throughout Germany uniform weights and measures. Throughout Germany a uniform currency. Nobody can make sense any more of this hotchpotch we're cluttered with. Here. The exact plan for the new money. (He hands around a plan) The mines are to be nationalized. The big capitalist combines are to be dissolved. We have three, four combines which control the entire market with their monopolies. A dozen people pocket in cash the entire proceeds of Germany's labor. A million of capital stock is quite sufficient. Anyone who has more must surrender half of it.

2ND DEPUTY   And if one of them earns a great deal?

1ST DEPUTY   He must lend the money to the cities, which can then give it at five per cent to the artisans. Then the middle class will get some of it too.

3RD DEPUTY   *(with the paper in his hand)* Sixty-three farthings—?

1ST DEPUTY   —equal to one new florin. 1 florin, half a florin, 1 quarter, half a quarter. The heller is to be called quarter, and the penny is to be called heller.

3RD DEPUTY   But the Austrian heller is worth two pence.

1ST DEPUTY   It becomes a penny.

2RD DEPUTY   But Mr. Deputy, a devaluation?

HIPLER   Please, gentlemen. Finance.

3RD DEPUTY   A financial reform is overdue. All imposts, duties, consumption taxes, escort dues, and so on will be abolished. Above all the internal customs dues of all these lords and lordships. No more customs. It only hinders trade and raises prices. One tax is enough. Perhaps we should still have a road tax, but then only for road building.

HIPLER   Home affairs?

5TH DEPUTY   *(holds up a thick volume)* One court of chancery as supreme court. Under it four high courts, sixteen state courts, sixty-four vehmic courts, and under them the city and village courts. President a noble, the majority of the co-judges citizens and peasants. The system of appeal is regulated as follows—

HIPLER   All complete, then?

5TH DEPUTY   In half a year it will be working.

2ND DEPUTY   I have one more question. What about the coins? What will they look like when all's done?

1ST DEPUTY   On one side the imperial eagle.

2ND DEPUTY   And on the other side?

1ST DEPUTY   That's the question.

2ND DEPUTY   The state prince's head?

1ST DEPUTY   I'm for the state arms.

2ND DEPUTY   But with the prince's head on the money, it gives it quite a different look.

1ST DEPUTY   And if the prince is deposed?

2ND DEPUTY   Oh, I see.

2ST DEPUTY   A coat of arms keeps longer.

2ND DEPUTY   But perhaps for Bavaria there could be a special regulation—

HIPLER   Gentlemen, please settle this in committee. I close the first session of the German Parliament.

(*On the platform there develops a busy to-and-fro of parliamentary business*)

TABLE LEFT FRONT

MÜNZER   The time passes. The time passes. Nothing happens. Now there they sit in Heilbronn and debate how they can do good to the princes. Oh holy simpletons!

PFEIFFER   But the princes do sign the treaties.

MÜNZER   The princes will sign anything until they have assembled their army. They should not believe them. Above all they should not make treaties with them. The lords will not keep a word of them.

PFEIFFER   We have the power everywhere.

MÜNZER   And make treaties and go home. So that the lords can deal with each state one by one.

PFEIFFER   Things must be done in an orderly fashion. A parliament after all is a great matter. Anything can be debated. The people will rule.

MÜNZER   Yes. But before they worry themselves about which prince's head to put on the coinage they should be worrying what to do with the princes' own actual heads.

PFEIFFER   No bloodshed.

MÜNZER   Here, the reports. The princes everywhere are assembling troops. No bloodshed. They'll turn Germany into a slaughterhouse and wipe their behinds with your treaties.

PFEIFFER   The majority wants to negotiate. There was a vote on it.

MÜNZER   I have often wondered why Christians are more afraid of their rulers than other peoples are. I think it must be because of the faint-hearted preachers.

PFEIFFER   Many still believe in Luther. And Luther is in favor of treaties.

MÜNZER   And in favor of censorship. So that my writings are not printed. Not because of my preaching, of course, but because of rebellion he would have me banished. A man may preach, but not change things. Isn't that clever? And how clever it is. The world will not notice for many years what murderous and treacherous havoc he has caused. But all the same it's a fine faith. He'll do much good yet. He'll serve up a very careful nation, I've no doubt.

PFEIFFER   You ask too much.

MÜNZER   The people must be brought to the very pitch of wonder and irritation if they are to be rid of their illusions and be properly instructed. The sort of wonder which rises in us as children, at six, seven years. When a man becomes aware of his origin. A new consciousness. A new man. That's what we need. This infatuation with possessions. This idolatry of houses and treasure-chambers. The lovely pewter utensils on the walls, the jewelry, silver and gold, the cash. If they only love that nothing will ever change. Why must we be affronted by this distorted reflection of a human being? Men should themselves be gods and realize heaven here on earth.

PFEIFFER   Men are men.

MÜNZER   There's no other way to attain the peace, the joy, and the justice which is their due. Is there? Lordship is the origin of all insurrection. If it isn't abolished, peace will be swamped. No people will ever believe their lord from that day forth. And the people cannot help the lord nor the lord the people. That is the origin of all death-dealing. The foolish world still mocks. It thinks it's still the old life. It goes on walking in its sleep till the water closes over its head. I tell you we must take good account of the new movement of the world today. The old assessments will fail utterly.

PFEIFFER   And those who have a use for this world, let them not mismuse it, for the substance of this world perishes.

MÜNZER   Bible, bubble, babble. (FRAU MÜNZER *enters, an infant on her arm*) My son. Thus are we caught up in civil life. Where are you off to?

FRAU MÜNZER   We're organizing a demonstration in the church, to annoy the priests. *(As she goes off)* Have you heard, in Salzungen the workers have expropriated the factories. Long live the revolution!

MÜNZER   We must see about the miners. Come on, Pfeiffer.

(MÜNZER *and* PFEIFFER *go off*)

PLATFORM RIGHT

(FREDERICK *in an armchair.* SPALATIN *is holding his hand. The* FOOL *is playing at executions with bones and skulls.*)

FREDERICK   I don't feel at all well today.

FOOL   You going to croak at last, you old hog's paunch?

FREDERICK   *(laughing)* What are you doing there?

FOOL   A merry old folk game. Eena meena mina mo and off you go. *(He knocks off a head)*

FREDERICK   Yes, the poor folk. So poor and headless. We princes are bad, Spalatin, very bad. We ought to ask God for forgiveness. Perhaps we've given the poor folk cause for such rebellion. These poorest ones. They are burdened by us in so many ways. It is true. We have done the good people wrong. A man does his best. Man proposes, God disposes. We'll leave it all in God's hands. Have the other gentlemen got their troops together at last?

SPALATIN   The deployment is complete.

FREDERICK   God will arrange everything nicely according to His will, and the peasants no doubt will soon be obedient again. But I want nothing to do with it. Nothing, nothing at all. I know nothing about it. *(He hoists himself up and goes off)* My dear Spalatin, if I should die, the sacrament in both kinds. Catholic and evangelical. For safety's sake. How should we know who is right? *(Goes off)*

FOOL   *(chopping off heads)* Eena meena mina mo and off you go. Eena meena mina mo and off you go.

SPALATIN   You'll soon have new toys.

FOOL   No. A new ruler and the old toys.

JOHN   *(coming onto the platform)* My brother's on his deathbed. I am taking over the government. A new wind, Spalatin, a keen and cutting wind. God will puff up his cheeks and give us a fine send-off. First of all we'll show this man Münzer where he gets off. We shall clean up without mercy. Is that understood?

SPALATIN   Perfectly.

JOHN   Send word to Luther. I expect from him an order of the day for the troops. But it must be absolutely first-rate. Something juicy. He knows the style.

SPALATIN   A hymn to God's lovely order.

JOHN   That's it, and I shall take over the supreme command. I'm expecting glorious victories. We're fighting after all against robbers and murderers.

SPALATIN   And blasphemers.

JOHN   That too. Issue the marching orders and see that beer is provided. *(He marches off singing)* Victorious we shall march— *(All go off)*

PLATFORM LEFT

(HIPLER *and the* DEPUTIES)

HIPLER   I open the second sitting of the German Parliament. Gentlemen, you know the situation is critical. An army of the princes has attacked our troops and massacred—yes, that's the word— four thousand peasants. The princes had a few horses wounded.

1ST DEPUTY   I propose that all castles and monasteries be occupied. The castles are points of support for the princes and a standing threat, besides which we need the weapons stocked there. If we want to keep the people together we also need the monastery supplies.

HIPLER   But that would put us outside the framework of law.

1ST DEPUTY   Which has already cost us four thousand peasants.

HIPLER   Officially we're still under truce. The negotiations with the princes could be endangered. Perhaps it was only a battalion commander exceeding orders.

2ND DEPUTY   After all, the princes have signed the treaties.

HIPLER   We must do everything we can to reach a friendly settlement. Even now, especially now. (1ST DEPUTY *goes off in a rage*) Point 1: In Weinsberg a noble was struck down and killed with his *lansquenets*. How could that happen?

3RD DEPUTY   A unique incident. In Leipheim they slaughtered four thousand and you get excited about an earl. I consider we should pass a vote of commendation to the peasants for their discipline.

HIPLER   The incident cannot be excused. The officer in charge. (OFFICER *steps forward*) What have you to say?

OFFICER   It happened against my orders and behind my back.

HIPLER   You had the responsibility.

OFFICER   The count wanted to set fire to the peasants' villages and drive out their women and children. The peasants were very excited, and besides that the news from Leipheim had just come in.

HIPLER   Is that all?

OFFICER   Yes.

HIPLER   You are demoted and will not return to your unit. (OFFICER *goes off. Everyone stands up. Silence*)

1ST DEPUTY   (*coming back*) The princes are attacking everywhere. They're burning down the villages. They're simply setting fire to the villages.

HIPLER   But they can't do that to us! They can't do that to us.

(*All the* DEPUTIES *go off*)

HIPLER   (*sits down. Pause*) They can't do that to us.

1ST DEPUTY   (*calling*) They're marching on Heilbronn!

HIPLER   (*waking up*) The constitution. Where is the constitution?

(*The* CLERK *gives it him.* HIPLER *is about to leave*)

CLERK   Herr Hipler, you still have to close the session.

HIPLER   What?

CLERK   The session has not been closed in due order.

HIPLER   I herewith close the second session of the German Parliament.

(*Both go off*)

TABLE LEFT FRONT

MÜNZER *(jumping onto the table)* Brothers! How much longer will you sleep! Oh, how often have I told you that it had to be. It is not possible while they live that you should be free of human fear. Nothing can be said to you about God so long as they rule over you. You must make a stand. If you do not, then your sacrifices are in vain. You will have to suffer all over again. Therefore be not faint-hearted, cease flattering the godless miscreants. Begin, fight, it is high time. Urge your brothers all to stand with you. Otherwise you must all perish. All Germany is awake, the master gamester wants to play with us, the miscreants must have their turn. They will beg you in friendly fashion, blubber, plead, like children. Don't let yourselves be moved to pity them. At them, at them, at them! It is time. It is beyond all measure a thing of highest need. At them, at them, at them, while the fire's still hot. Don't let your sword grow cold. Throw their tower to the ground. At them, at them, at them, so long as you have daylight. At them, at them, at them! *(He jumps down from the table. Adherents gather around him)*

TABLE RIGHT FRONT

LUTHER *(on the table)* Faithless, perjured, disobedient, rebels, murderers, robbers, blasphemers, I think there is no devil left in hell, they have all got into the peasants. Therefore let whoever can strike home, strangle, stab, secretly or publicly, and remember there can be nothing more poisonous, harmful, or more devilish than a rebellious person, to be struck down like a mad dog. Therefore there can be no sleeping here. Here is no place for patience or pity. It is the time of the sword and of anger, not of mercy. Authority must strike home with good conscience as long as one muscle still twitches. For here is the advantage, that the peasants have bad consciences and an unjust cause. And any peasant who is slaughtered in that cause belongs body and soul to the Devil forevermore. But authority has a good conscience and a just cause. Such wonderful times are with us now that a prince can better serve Heaven by shedding blood than others by prayer. Therefore, dear lords, save here, rescue here, help here, pity the poor folk. Stab, strike, strangle, whoever can. If you get your death by it, well for you. A more blessed death you can never earn. For you will die in the service of love. Here let every pious man say *Christ Amen*. For the prayer is right and good and well-pleasing to God. That I know. *(He climbs down from the table)*

TABLE LEFT FRONT

(The MÜNZER ADHERENTS *have gathered. They link arms, march to the rear in a broad front, and sing.)*
Come, Holy Ghost, Lord God.

(PFEIFFER *remains behind*)

FRAU MÜNZER *(dashing onto the stage from left)* Pfeiffer! The workers. They're not coming. They have been promised an increase of wages.

(PFEIFFER *looks back at the demonstrators, then he takes* FRAU MÜNZER *by the arm, both go off quickly. From the background rifle fire and salvos of cannon. The singing stops. Quiet)*

PLATFORM RIGHT

POPE Religions are no use. Completely superfluous. I should know. I am the Pope.

CAJETAN The new religion is called science. Why believe when you can know?

BIBBIENA What that Luther there has written, it's medieval.

CAJETAN And nothing new at all. Hundreds of others have written that. Huss, Wessel, Ganzfort, Goch, Savonarola, Johann von Wesel.

POPE The Germans always notice everything a hundred years too late. The earth is expanding. The heavens are changing. Everywhere there's movement. A new spirit is entering people's heads. Then this fellow discovers the Bible. It's incredible. A provincial from Saxony. A German professor. What does he actually want? Can one person tell me what he wants?

BIBBIENA To be right.

POPE To be right about one thing he would rather plunge the world into misfortune?

(BIBBIENA *shrugs his shoulders*)

To be right. What right? Whose right? What is right? Oh God, this God of theirs! We should do better to concern ourselves with the earth. The finest planet. First prize: peace on earth. Instead of that we shall now be having a regular, stand-up, dogmatic fight about who has the only true, hundred-per-cent right and really loving God. And in five hundred years we shall note that not one of us is right, and then at last we shall stand where we stand today. I could go and hang myself. (*He gets up, to* CAJE-TAN) So throw your Copernicus away. (*To* BIBBIENA) And Michelangelo had better see who is to pay for his marble. (BIB-BIENA *hands him a long black priest's cassock. He puts it on*) Back into the lap of the Church. We wear our skirts long and become Christians again. A fine uniform. Can one of you do the mass?

BIBBIENA   (*offended*) I am a Cardinal, not a priest.

POPE   I didn't become a priest till I was already Pope, and then I had no more time. How did it go—consecration of the Host— Somebody must be left in Rome who can still do the mass.

CAJETAN   I shouldn't be too sure. (*He gives him a fat book*)

POPE   What's that?

CAJETAN   The Bible.

POPE   (*clapping the Bible shut—a cloud of dust*) Incense I always imagined differently. (*Loudly*) I believe in God, the Almighty Father, creator of Heaven and earth— (*All go off*)

PLATFORM LEFT

(ERASMUS *at a high desk.* HOLBEIN *is painting him.* PARA-CELSUS *comes onto the platform.*)

PARACELSUS   Holbein paints Erasmus, and Erasmus writes a poem about Holbein. A cozy time you have in Basel.

HOLBEIN   Do up your breeches before you open your mouth.

PARACELSUS   (*to* ERASMUS) Your leg. I have something new. (ERASMUS *stretches out a leg to him.* PARACELSUS *rubs an ointment into the leg*) What's art doing?

ERASMUS   Rhyming. And science?

PARACELSUS   Inventing ointments. (*To* HOLBEIN) I hear the people of Basel are getting you to do the paintings for their city hall.
HOLBEIN   So do I.
PARACELSUS   Evangelical or Catholic?
HOLBEIN   With paints.
PARACELSUS   You painters have an easy life. (ERASMUS *takes up a manuscript and starts correcting it*) A new book?
ERASMUS   I've been working at it for five years.
PARACELSUS   Writers are funny. They think about a thing for five years, and what do they do then? They write a book about it.
ERASMUS   Physicians are funny creatures. They treat the sick even when they're drunk.
PARACELSUS   I have to treat drunk patients.

(FROBENIUS *comes onto the platform loaded with manuscripts*)

FROBENIUS   God be with you, Master Paracelsus.
PARACELSUS   God be with you, Master Frobenius.
PROBENIUS   Do you like it in Switzerland?
PARACELSUS   I'll say I do! (*To* ERASMUS) I've heard you must know the dialect if you want to become a citizen.
ERASMUS   English is enough.
PARACELSUS   Are you staying in Basel?
ERASMUS   They let a man write here. These days that's a lot.
FROBENIUS   In Germany they're wrangling. Will it spread across the frontier? It's a problem for me. As a publisher I want wrangles because they produce books. As a Swiss citizen I want peace. As a man I'm between the two and don't rightly know. If we could only get clear about God.
PARACELSUS   Religion is only waste of time. Every morning you have to stick your head out a window and look to see if the air is Evangelical or Catholic and which word of God happens to be overhead at the moment darkening the sky. At every turnpike you have to change your religion like your money. In one city you're a believer, in the next a heretic. In a hundred years they'll be laughing at us. Nobody will be talking about God any more.
ERASMUS   God grant it.
FROBENIUS   Do you really think that, Master Paracelsus?
PARACELSUS   Master Frobenius, I tell you: there is no God.

FROBENIUS Master Paracelsus, you're a bold man. I admire you.
(*To* ERASMUS) I have here the new galleys. Is this right? *(He
reads)* "I have always wanted to be alone and hate nothing so
much as sworn partisans."

ERASMUS Yes.

FROBENIUS "I should like to be a citizen of the world, on a common
footing with everyone, or better still a stranger to everyone."

ERASMUS Yes.

FROBENIUS "Nationalism is one of the curses of humanity. The
politicians' task must be to found a world state. It is better to
speak of people and things in such a way that we consider this
world as our common fatherland."

ERASMUS Yes.

FROBENIUS "Opinions which have taken root among us can be
sooner expunged from consciousness by disputing about them
with well-grounded arguments than by mere assertions."

ERASMUS Yes.

FROBENIUS "All wars are started in the interest of the rulers and
always waged to the disadvantage of the people. Rulers and gen-
erals may derive profit from war, while the great masses have to
bear its costs and its misfortunes. A peace is never so unjust as
not to be preferable to the most just war."

ERASMUS Yes.

FROBENIUS "Those who deny the existence of God are not so
impious as those who represent Him as inexorable."

ERASMUS Yes.

FROBENIUS Well, thank Heaven for that, all correct, and here was
I thinking the compositors had been playing a trick on me. They
are such unusual thoughts.

ERASMUS You can throw it all away now. Reason, enlightenment,
and toleration are no longer in demand.

FROBENIUS Perhaps it will yet be taken up one day.

ERASMUS Our cause is lost. For centuries. For people like us there
are bad times coming in Germany.

FROBENIUS Will there be war?

ERASMUS Undoubtedly. Germany in two different camps, what
else should come of that but war?

FROBENIUS This Luther—

ERASMUS   Never utter that name again. I can no longer bear to hear
it. Look at Wittenberg and look at Rome, Florence, Paris, Brussels, London, Basel, Amsterdam. There you know it all. For a time
it was our turn. The Pope, the Emperor, the kings of England
and France listened to me, even the German princes. But the
time was too short. It didn't suffice.

PARACELSUS   Is writing enough?

ERASMUS   Is painting enough?

HOLBEIN   Is science enough?

PARACELSUS   Is money-getting enough?

FROBENIUS   May I invite the gentlemen to a glass of red wine?

(All go off)

CENTER STAGE FOOTLIGHTS

(FUGGER, CHARLES, *and a* HERALD—*without fanfare.*)

FUGGER   May I congratulate you on your victory over France?
Young man, Eruope belongs to you.

CHARLES   If you'll give me a hundred, I'll invite you to dinner.

FUGGER   Thrift, young man, thrift. Your grandfather ended just that
way.

CHARLES   A five.

FUGGER   Unfortunately I never carry change. (*To the* HERALD)
Are we ready then?

HERALD   With fanfare?

FUGGER   Not for me. Plain and simple.

HERALD   It is after all an act of state.

FUGGER   Very good then.

HERALD   In such cases we blow—

FUGGER   *You* are the expert.

(*The* HERALD *takes up his position. On one side* FUGGER,
on the other CHARLES)

HEARALD   Fanfare. Three times long, six times short, plain . . .

FUGGER   Where have you—

CHARLES   Pawned.

HERALD   (*reading a document*) We, Charles, Emperor by God's

Grace. To all and sundry. Mines are the greatest gift which Almighty God has given us, because a great treasure of gold, silver, copper, tin, quicksilver, iron, and other metals is won from them, many people by their work in them gain their necessitous livelihood, and greatly increase the income of the princes and lords, so that the mining industry must be pushed forward by all possible means. For the greater the profit for the lords and princes, the greater the profit for the commonalty. If on the other hand this support is neglected, the economy will quite certainly go to ruin and the commonalty will suffer harm. Of all the provisions and means by which the economy can be sumptuously, fruitfully, and also durably maintained, operated, furthered, and also increased, none is more useful and reliable than to keep prices high by a good system of control and not to sell the products cheap. Therefore the products must not be produced and marketed by many people, but everything must be put in the hands of one single person or at most a few persons, who produce, process, and sell it. This has already been the custom since— (*To* FUGGER) Since when?

FUGGER   For forty years.

HERALD   —for some forty years. That is in other lands the case and still happens daily, and so it is good. For where the goods are sold at high prices, which is best achieved by the concentration in one man's hands, the others too become cheerful, and therewith the common good is furthered and increased. Thus the sinking of mines and the extraction of metals is a thing like other gifts of God with which a person may be endowed, and to process, buy, and sell these goods is a godly, honorable, and permissible activity, and it is only fitting to give all help to those honorable persons who put their capital into mines and so often and so grievously miscalculate in doing so, and apart from their participation have nothing but their good hopes, in order to keep them well disposed. For gold, silver, and other metals are not goods which form part of an ordinary man's necessities. And if the prices are high the workers should take comfort, for it is certain that then wages too are high. One thing however is certain, if we do not procure the capital in this way the goods will certainly become very, very scarce, and that would be harmful to the commonalty. So we lay down, order, declare, and desire out of our own consummate power and with good conscience that in all places all goods, especially mines and metals, be concentrated in the hands of a few— (FUGGER *nudges him in the ribs*) — in a single hand, and that those who then possess everything can sell the goods at the highest prices, entirely according to their pleasure. Therefore it is decreed that what in future will come about according to proclamation of the concentration of all goods in the hands of a few is no unseemly action, nor is it to be called monopoly, nor even considered such, and still less has anyone to justify himself in the sight of others because of such activities. He may not be punished nor complained of by anyone, irrespective of whether it is considered or understood as disadvantageous by some few persons. And if we have ever anywhere enacted a prohibition of monopolies, or shall in future enact one, then all monopolies are to be excepted from it, and so we order all our subjects, under pain of our displeasure and heavy punishment, to observe this new economic order and not to tolerate anything contrary. *(He rolls up the document)* Fanfare. Four times long, twice short. Plain. (FUGGER *takes the document*

CHARLES   Am I to abdicate right now or not till later?

FUGGER   How so? You do your job very creditably. We need good men in the administration too.

(All go off)

TABLE RIGHT FRONT

(At the table sits a PEASANT.)

1ST MERCENARY   *(enters, singing)*

> Were my mother a whore
> My father a thief
> Yet if I had money
> I'd know no grief.

Fine times, eh?

PEASANT   The Lord give your nags a long life, or they'll yet be riding at us.

1ST MERCENARY   I don't think the masters will slaughter everyone.

Certainly not everyone. Otherwise they'd have to live alone on the earth.

PEASANT   Yes.

1ST MERCENARY   *(singing)*

> Were my mother a whore
> My father a thief
> Yet if I had money
> I'd know no grief.

That Luther daren't show his face to the people any more, eh?

PEASANT   No.

1ST MERCENARY   Were you one of Münzer's men?

PEASANT   Yes.

1st MERCENARY   For every Münzer adherent captured we get five florins. He is then tortured and finally killed. Perhaps we could do a different kind of deal. After the battle of Pavia I was able to sell the corpse of a duke. To the family. For a Christian burial, consecrated ground and so on. A thing like that brings in money, more than a five. Supposing the family has any.

PEASANT   I understand.

1ST MERCENARY   It's true it would be a hand-of-honor deal. You have to be able to trust your man.

PEASANT   Yes. I see that.

1ST MERCENARY   Have you anything?

PEASANT   Yes.

1ST MERCENARY   A good amount?

PEASANT   I have a few houses in the town.

1ST MERCENARY   Family?

PEASANT   That too.

1ST MERCENARY   Family vault?

PEASANT   Yes.

1ST MERCENARY   The torture is very cruel. And then to be hanged anyway at the end of it. So a quick death would be preferable. I'm a good hand at that.

PEASANT   Yes.

1ST MERCENARY   So you see, brother, you have a nice death, I get my money and am a merciful fellow in the bargain. A Christian deal.

PEASANT   Yes.

1ST MERCENARY   (*drawing a knife and giving the* PEASANT *his hand*) Brother.
PEASANT   Brother.
1ST MERCENARY   The money. You understand.
PEASANT   Yes.
1ST MERCENARY   (*stabs him, The* PEASANT *falls on his face. The* MERCENARY *draws out the knife, wipes it clean and sings*)

> Were my mother a whore
> My father a thief
> Yet if I had money
> I'd know no grief.

TABLE LEFT FRONT

(*Two* MERCENARIES, *each with a corpse on his shoulder, come forward.*)

MERCENARIES   (*calling*) Corpses for sale, corpses for sale! (*They throw the corpses onto the ground*)
1ST MERCENARY   (*drags his peasant over*) I'm in luck. I've caught another house-owner.
2ND MERCENARY   Hope we haven't set fire to it.
1ST MERCENARY   At least he'll have money. (*Some* WOMEN *come on from left. They look over the men*)
1ST WOMAN   That's mine.
2ND MERCENARY   Twenty florins.
1ST WOMAN   Twenty?
2ND MERCENARY   Look, it's still standing. (*He kicks the penis*) If you put him to bed quick, you can still have a go.
1ST WOMAN   Ten florins.
2ND MERCENARY   Fifteen, or I'll chop him into mincemeat. (1ST WOMAN *pays and drags the corpse away*)
3RD MERCENARY   Yours?
2ND WOMAN   (*nods*)
3RD MERCENARY   Twenty.
2ND WOMAN   I have no money.
3RD WOMAN   Everything's missing. No arms or legs.
3RD MERCENARY   Easier to carry that way.

2ND WOMAN   I have no money.

3RD MERCENARY   Good, as he's somewhat damaged, ten.

2ND WOMAN   I have no money.

3RD MERCENARY   (*chops off the corpse's head*) Badly damaged. Five.

2ND WOMAN   No money.

3RD MERCENARY   Then I'll throw him into the river.

1ST MERCENARY   And this one?

3RD WOMAN   He's not one of ours.

1ST MERCENARY   You trying to fool me? He has houses.

3RD WOMAN   He's quite unknown here.

1ST MERCENARY   The swine has cheated me.

> (*The* MERCENARIES *drag the dead off to the rear.* 1ST MERCENARY *sings*)

> Were my mother a whore
> My father a thief
> Yet if I had money
> I'd know no grief.

TABLE RIGHT FRONT

MELANCHTHON   I feel quite ill.

LUTHER   It doesn't affect me at all. I'm a rough peasant, and I have become thick-skinned in such matters by nature. I hope they won't be long. I want to get married today.

MELANCHTHON   *What* do you want?

LUTHER   To get married.

MELANCHTHON   What? Now? With all Germany swimming in blood?

LUTHER   What of it? —The Princes.

> (*From right* JOHN, ALBERT, *and a few* PRINCES *enter.* MELAN-CHTHON *and* LUTHER *bow.*)

LUTHER   Most serene, high-born, all-gracious princes and lords. There are some of you who say this is the fruit of my teaching. Then you do not know what I have taught and what the gospel is. Those who rightly read and understand my teaching do not make rebellion; they don't have it from me. You must bear witness that

I have taught in all tranquility, have vigorously opposed rebellion, and have zealously urged and warned your subjects to be obedient to authority even when it was rabid and tyrannical, and so this rebellion cannot come from me. Nobody has so resisted and withstood it as I. If I can no longer hold back the mob, how am I or my gospel to blame for that, when we've always prayed for you, protected your sovereignty, and helped to preserve it among the people? From the beginning I have absolutely and always taught that the civil order must be maintained. Therefore freely continue to wield the sword. It is necessary and God wills it that fear and terror be brought among the people, so that the peasants in future know how wrong they are. No need to be too punctilious. If there are innocent people among them, no doubt God will save them. If He does not do so, then they are not innocent. I am of opinion it is better that all the peasants should be slaughtered than that anything should happen to the princes. If I were a lord, I would strike out and slaughter them all. Therefore don't let yourselves grow soft. Authority must strike out so that they hold their tongues and realize that it is serious. If they say it is too severe to stop their mouths like that with violence, I say it is right. Such mouths must be answered with the fist. The peasants wouldn't listen, so their ears had to be unstopped with bullets, so that their heads were blown to pieces. Whoever will not hear God's word must feel the executioner. I want to hear nothing of mercy. Authority cannot and must not be merciful.

JOHN   Counsel Melanchthon we hope is also of this opinion?

MELANCHTHON   It goes without saying that I am of this opinion. Decrees of authority are among God's good created things and it is sinful to disregard them. I have prepared an affidavit. (He hands over the affidavit) All demands of the peasants are illegal. Even though they were in the right with their articles. The peasants must give up their farms to the lords. The farms no longer belong to them but God has given them to the lords. An authority often has cause to take away other men's lands, to fence them in or for any other purpose. And although this is violence, it is wrong to resist it.

1ST PRINCE   And the taxes? The peasants allege that we do not put them to proper use.

MELANCHTHON That is no concern of the people's; they must give what dues are imposed upon them.

2ND PRINCE And serfdom?

MELANCHTHON It is outrage and violence that they should not want to be serfs. The serfs should be obedient to their masters in fear and trembling. Yes, it seems necessary that such a wild and unruly people as the Germans should have less freedom than they now have. Our gentry permit the folk all kinds of wantonness, only take money from it, and do not hold it under discipline. It must be governed much more severely. God calls the secular government a sword. But a sword should cut. It is much too merciful only to impose fines. God says "Thou shalt show no mercy." To pith them would mean denying God, blaspheming against Him, and seeking to cast Him down from Heaven.

JOHN I think once more there's a substantial salary rise due here. (LUTHER *and* MELANCHTHON *bow*)

LUTHER Your Electoral Highness sees that the world cannot be ruled solely with force; there must be learned folk who help with God's word to keep the people in check. If there were no teachers and preachers the secular power would not stand for long.

JOHN (*placing himself between* MELANCHTHON *and* LUTHER *and putting his arms on their shoulders*) Well, gentlemen, what do you say? These are my dear young friends.

LUTHER We pray to God that we may long continue to hold the towel to our princes, and that beasts and peasants do not become our princes.

JOHN And what shall we do with the property of the Church?

LUTHER If Your Electoral Highness wishes to continue to be of use to God and His faithful instrument, Your Electoral Highness will find the means to do it there. There are enough monasteries, foundations, fiefs, charities, and suchlike things, if only Your Electoral Highness would care to give orders, to inspect, calculate, and make dispositions. It all now comes into the hands of Your Electoral Highness as our supreme head. God will give it His blessing.

ALBERT And what shall I do? I'm a Cardinal. I only have bishoprics.

LUTHER Your Grace should marry, like me. Marry, appoint yourself a secular prince, confiscate your own Church estates, and transform the whole state into a hereditary princedom.

ALBERT   My my my, what will the ordinary people say to that?

LUTHER   The pastors must skillfully lead the common man up to the question whether it would not be better for Your Grace to exchange the hypocrisy of ecclesiastical life for marriage and transform the confusion of bishoprics into one fine princedom. After that it must come before the public, and when the people in its turn puts this idea to Your Grace and humbly begs it, Your Grace declares that the people have convinced you and that you will meet their wishes.

ALBERT   Oh, that's how it goes! Well then, all power to the people. *(He laughs)*

JOHN   It's we who make the revolution.

(MELANCHTHON *goes off.* ALBERT *takes* LUTHER *aside*)

ALBERT   May I offer you a purse of gold? Only a trifle. For your favors.

LUTHER   No, no question of it. I never take anything.

ALBERT   Let's say for your wedding.

LUTHER   On no account. I take nothing. Give it to my wife.

(FRAU LUTHER *comes up*)

ALBERT   Gracious lady. *(Kisses her hand)*

FRAU LUTHER   *(court curtsey)* Most gracious lord. (ALBERT *gives her the purse of gold.* LUTHER *and* FRAU LUTHER *go off left*)

LUTHER   *(in a low voice)* How much?

FRAU LUTHER   *(testing the weight of the purse in her hand)* Two thousand.

(*An* OFFICER *has entered right, behind him a few* LANS-QUENETS *with* MÜNZER *bound*)

JOHN   How many?

OFFICER   Six thousand dead.

JOHN   Quite nice for one afternoon. Well, and so this is Münzer. How was it? All men are equal?

MÜNZER   *(exhausted)* All men are equal.

JOHN   Well well, all men are equal. *(He kicks him in the belly)*

2ND PRINCE   All men are equal? *(He hits him)*
3RD PRINCE   All men are equal? *(He kicks him)*
4TH PRINCE   All men are equal? *(He hits him)*
PRINCES   Equal, equal, equal, equal, equal. *(Beat him all together.*
MÜNZER *is left lying, does not rise. The* LANSQUENETS *drag
him to the center of the stage)*
EXECUTIONER   *(entering)* There are some women here, begging for
mercy on their husbands.
JOHN   Mercy? Well, what shall we do? If I show mercy, I am a
sinner. Who wants to be a sinner? Have we still got a few cap-
tains?
EXECUTIONER   Yes.
JOHN   Then later, when we're at our celebration dinner, the women
shall beat out their brains. That'll teach them to have ideas. But I
must see the brains spatter, otherwise they'll not get their husbands back. *(To* ALBERT) That's how you become a sinner.
From pure compassion. The people can never make that good.
*(*ALBERT *and the other* PRINCES *mount the platform)*
EXECUTIONER   If I may in all humility submit my account.
JOHN   Yet another executioner's account?
3RD PRINCE   I already have a whole pocketful of them myself.
JOHN   But itemized. Not all mixed up. Order. Beheaded, hanged,
quartered, broken on the wheel, drowned, burned. And no paper
corpses to be included, such as died under torture.
EXECUTIONER   Already deducted. Twelve hundred eighteen
beheaded.
JOHN   I pay one florin.
EXECUTIONER   Broken on the wheel, quartered, drowned, in all—
JOHN   I'm not paying those; that's sadism.
EXECUTIONER   Eight hundred thirty-one, eyes put out.
JOHN   Half a florin.
EXECUTIONER   Seven hundred and eleven, tongue torn out.
JOHN   Ditto.
EXECUTIONER   Nine hundred and ten, hands chopped off.
JOHN   Ditto.
EXECUTIONER   Various children, eyes put out and tongues torn
out.
JOHN   I'm not paying for children.

EXECUTIONER   Your Electoral Highness will all the longer have subjects who are blind and dumb.

JOHN   That's an argument. *(He takes the account)* Then people are surprised that our administration costs are so high.

(He goes onto the platform to join the other PRINCES. *The* EXE-CUTIONER *goes over to stage center by* MÜNZER)

PLATFORM RIGHT

3RD PRINCE   It was a good haul. I shall have to follow it up at once with a pilgrimage or a pious foundation.

1ST PRINCE   My peasants surrendered at once, threw themselves on my mercy. Without arms, bareheaded, and barefoot they came to meet us, white rods in folded hands. Then we charged them and cleaned up. Eighteen thousand peasants. I can still see the picture, the folded hands, the white rods, the red blood. White and red. Like my state colors. I like it, it looks so fresh.

2ND PRINCE   I do it this way. I take the peasants prisoner, then free them for ransom, take them prisoner again and destroy them. That way you have them dead and their money as well. Otherwise they'll always hide something.

3RD PRINCE   I left them lying three days without bread or water in the ditch by my castle, so that they fought over the dishwater. It was terribly funny.

4TH PRINCE   In my case they took refuge in the church. So I set fire to it, and they were all burned. And the funniest part of it was that to the very end they sang hymns to God. *(They all laugh)*

JOHN   God the Almighty is as ever on the side of the rulers.

ALBERT   They were really quite nice people. So obliging, so polite, and so submissive; I cannot really say anything bad about them. *(The* PRINCES *look at him. An embarrassed silence)* You know this one, a bishop comes naked out of the confessional— *(Pause)* Now I've forgotten it.

JOHN   So with God's help we have conquered and therewith accomplished a good work. So let us all be thankful to the Almighty. *(They pray)*

PLATFORM LEFT

(FRAU LUTHER *is knitting,* LUTHER *is sorting papers.*)

FRAU LUTHER   Dearest, what does *non putassem* mean?

LUTHER   *Non putassem?* I should never have thought it. The ancients consider it the most disgraceful thing a man can say. For it indicates a cocksure, stubborn, careless man who in one moment, with one step, with one word can do more harm than ten men like him can make good. And then after it all he will say, I really should. never have thought it.

FRAU LUTHER   That's a thing I should never have thought.

LUTHER   *(slapping his hand down on a document)* Münzer here, they didn't put the right questions to him under torture. I should have had him questioned quite differently. This is not a confession. He declares that he did nothing evil. It's enough to make you cry with rage. Nothing evil. I shouldn't have thought it possible that a human heart could be so hardened.

FRAU LUTHER   Münzer's a wicked man, is he?

LUTHER   A very wicked man.

FRAU LUTHER   *Non putassem.*

LUTHER   This morning I was out in the country and asked the peasants why they no longer pay their pastors, their soulherds, when they'd pay their cowherds right enough. Do you know what they said? We need our cowherds. It's gone as far as that. The world is choking in sin.

FRAU LUTHER   *Non putassem.*

LUTHER   They simply refuse to give anything any more. There is such ingratitude among the common folk for the holy word of God, without doubt a plague sent upon them by God. They live like swine. No fear of God any more. I'm already regretting having freed them as I did from the tyrants. They're ungrateful beasts. They don't deserve the treasure of the gospel. We should not cast pearls before swine.

FRAU LUTHER   Don't vex yourself. Make a little song.

LUTHER   You're right. *(He starts composing on a sheet of paper)*

FRAU LUTHER   It's certain, I suppose, the folk will all be thinking badly of you now?

LUTHER   Let them. I know how to extricate myself and leave them sticking in the mud. *(He hums a song)*

FRAU LUTHER   Well, yes, we've made a good thing of it.

LUTHER   Yes.

FRAU LUTHER   I don't know why people so abuse the Prince. Such a nice gentleman! He's given us the monastery.

LUTHER   It doesn't bring in as much as it used to.

FRAU LUTHER   It's big, and I'll open a guest house. You're famous. A lot of people will come, and we can collect a handsome boarding fee.

LUTHER   Yes.

FRAU LUTHER   He's raised your salary too.

LUTHER   Fifty thousand.

FRAU LUTHER   And then he gave us a fine sum as an extra present.

LUTHER   Sixty thousand.

FRAU LUTHER   With that we can buy a fine farm. It'll be a good investment.

LUTHER   Yes, farms are cheap now.

FRAU LUTHER   And then we'll buy a fishpond too, a vineyard, and a few large gardens. And don't forget the monastery has brewery rights. You're a master brewer now. Martin Luther, the great master brewer of Wittenberg. *Non putassem. (She laughs vigorously)* And then we'll get a coat of arms, and we'll build a new entrance gate onto the monastery, with your portrait and your coat of arms. A fine new façade. *(She laughs)*

LUTHER   Yes. It's become serious now. Now is the time to keep still and let God take over. *(Pause. He composes)* Preachers are the greatest killers of all. I, Martin Luther, have massacred all the peasants in the revolt. I gave orders to kill them. All their blood is on my head. But I put it off onto our Lord God, it was He who commanded me to speak such things. Whoever weighs and tests these matters carefully has learned something.

CENTER FOOTLIGHTS

(FUGGER *is kneeling at his prie-dieu.* SCHWARZ *lays the ac-*

count book open on the prie-dieu and lights two candles to the left and right of it)

FUGGER   *(folding his hands)* The end.

SCHWARZ   Balance of the firm Jacob Fugger. Total: 203,265,200. That is a profit of over a thousand per cent.

FUGGER   They were good years. Praised be Capital.

SCHWARZ   For ever and ever. Amen.

FUGGER   O Capital!

SCHWARZ   Have mercy upon us.

FUGGER

> Thou beginning and end of all things.
> That wert and art and shalt be.
> From which, through which, and in which everything is.
> In which we live, move, and have our being.
> Which has all power, in the heavens and upon earth.
> And has the keys of hell and of death.
> That has ordered everything by number, weight, and measure.
> Thou king of kings and lord of lords.
> Whose majesty fills the earth.
> Whose wisdom mightily rules and orders all things.

SCHWARZ   Have mercy upon us.

FUGGER   O Capital!

SCHWARZ   Deliver us.

FUGGER

> From thy wrath.
> From unbelief and superstition.
> From littleness of spirit and overweening arrogance toward thee.
> From mistrust of thy loving providence.
> From complaining against thy wise decrees.
> From all disparagement of thy most high majesty.
> Through thy eternal might and wisdom.
> Through thy riches.

SCHWARZ   Deliver us.

FUGGER   O Capital!
SCHWARZ   We beseech thee.
FUGGER

> That all men may believe in thee.
> That all may acknowledge and worship thee as
> their creator.
> That all may praise and esteem thy holy name.
> That all may faithfully perform thy holy will.
> That all may love thee from their hearts as
> their highest good.
> That thou shouldst lead us into thy kingdom,
> which thou hast prepared for them that are thine.
> That we submit ourselves like children to all
> thy dispensations.
> That it may please thee to bless our labors
> and affairs.
> That it may please thee to strengthen and
> maintain us in thy holy service.
> That it may please thee to admit us to the
> inheritance of thy eternal kingdom.

SCHWARZ   We beseech thee to hear us.
FUGGER   O Capital!
SCHWARZ   Have mercy upon us.
FUGGER

> Thou goal and end of all creatures.
> Thou terror of the poor.
> Thou joy of the rich.
> Thou cause of our cheerfulness.
> Thou refuge of sinners.
> Thou food of the elect.
> Thou source of all grace.
> With the divine word united in substance.
> Thou tabernacle of the all highest.
> Thou abyss of all virtues.
> Thou center of all hearts.
> Thou salvation of those who put their hopes in
> thee.
> Thou hope of those who die in thee.

SCHWARZ   Have mercy upon us.
FUGGER   O Capital!

SCHWARZ   We beseech thee to hear us.
FUGGER

> Through thy victory over all thy enemies.
> Through eternal might and glory.
> That it may please thee to maintain us in thy favor.
> That it may please thee to bring into the way of truth all such as have erred and are deceived.
> That it may please thee to fulfill thy works among all the peoples of the earth.
> That it may please thee to guide all our thoughts, words, and deeds according to thy good pleasure.
> That it may please thee to admit us into the company of the elect.
> That it may please thee to maintain and increase in us faith and veneration toward thee.
> That it may please thee to kindle in us a fervent love of thee.
> That it may please thee to arouse in us the craving for more frequent enjoyment of thee

SCHWARZ   We beseech thee to hear us.
FUGGER   All saints.
SCHWARZ   Pray for us.
FUGER

> Debits and credits.
> Interest and dividends.
> Bills and checks.
> Discount and Dow Jones.
> Stocks and shares.
> Mortgages and depreciations.
> Limited liability and joint stock companies.
> Taxes and repayments.
> Investments and real estate.
> Foreign exchange and money market.
> Boom and slump.
> Gold and diamonds.
> Inflation and deflation.
> Credit and speculation.
> Business conditions and balance sheets.

SCHWARZ   Pray for us.
FUGGER

> Ye who worship and adore it without end.
> Sing holy, holy, holy.
> Ye who harken to its voice and do its will with rejoicing.
> Ye who proclaim its decrees to mankind.
> Ye who are sent forth in its service.
> Ye who accompany and protect us in all our journeys.
> Grant that we may follow your promptings and at all times faithfully do your will.
> Grant that we may venerate you together with our Lord Capital.
> Grant that we may eternally praise Capital together with you.

SCHWARZ   Pray for us.
FUGGER

> Thou comfort of the rich.
> Thou light of millionaires.
> Thou fire of the poor.
> Thou joy of shareholders.
> Thou illuminator of governments.
> Thou inspiration of prophets.
> Thou strength of managers.
> Thou purity of harlots.
> Thou bliss of heirs.
> O thou surfeited with ignominy.

SCHWARZ   Deliver us.
FUGGER

> From the agonizing reproaches of conscience.
> From the great affliction.
> From the terrible darkness.
> From the dread wailing and gnashing of teeth.
> From the sorrowful destitution.

O Capital, who taketh upon Thyself the sins of the world.
Give us eternal peace.

(*At the end of the* FUGGER *litany,* LUTHER, FRAU LUTHER, *and the* PRINCES *rise and sing*)

> God is a stronghold and a tower,
> A help that never faileth,
> A covering shield, a sword of power,
> When Satan's host assaileth.
> In vain our crafty foe
> Still strives to work us woe,
> Still lurks and lies in wait
> With more than earthly hate;
> We will not faint, nor tremble.
>
> Our Father's truth abideth sure;
> Christ, our Redeemer, liveth;
> For us he pleads his offering pure,
> To us his Spirit giveth.
> Though dear ones pass away,
> Though strength and life decay,
> Yet loss shall be our gain,
> For God doth still remain
> Our All-in-all for ever.

(*During the hymn they walk down from the platforms and station themselves in a row in the center of the stage. With their gowns, which they draw out wide, they conceal the execution of* MÜN-ZER. *Behind their backs cries of pain are heard. They sing louder. An axe strikes the block. They sing still louder.* MÜNZER'S *head, stuck on a long pole, emerges from behind their backs and looks down into the auditorium. They sing still louder.* FUGGER *prays. Curtain.*)

On my method

This play is not about theology. The theological aspect of the Reformation has for four hundred years been again and again investigated in innumerable books. The social consequences of these events have hardly been noticed. Yet we are still feeling them today.

Nor is this play about ideological testimonies. You cannot make a play out of ready-made answers and assumed opinions.

It is about four young people. One of them was called Luther, one Münzer, the two others Karlstadt and Melanchthon. It is about the invention of bookkeeping. It is about the first great German revolution. That the two coincide is perhaps not a matter of chance.

Its subject therefore was the concrete investigation of a situation. The play covers the years 1514–1525. That the references to our time are so clear and unmistakeable was a surprise to me. There was no need to actualize or to twist confrontations for theatrical effects. It seems there are in history combinations of circumstances which repeat themselves like models.

I have worked on this subject for five years. I had no secret sources at my disposal. I read and thoroughly studied the available material over its entire range. I have, it is true, allowed myself to examine closely the entanglement of ecclesiastical history with political and economic history. One of the principal reasons why the play is so long is that the original texts are incorporated, and placed in their proper context. The speeches are not just assembled haphazardly, but taken from the writings which deal with a particular theme. Moreover the chronological order has been preserved. When Luther adopts a given view, the sentences are not thrown together, but I have used his letters and writings from that period about those events. There are a very few—well-founded—exceptions. When it is a question of differences and discussion of principle, the utterances fundamental to such a question are inserted. Where I was in doubt, I have given expression to my doubt, or else I have entirely deleted the scenes concerned. I have in every case relied on recognized "translations." Naturally, medieval texts cannot be used word for word.

That Luther comes out of it differently from the man we knew will no doubt be painful for many. But they are after all his own words. If Münzer seems too much a man of today, that is not my doing. That Fugger was not a "helper of mankind" but one who made money out of mankind should not be put down to me. It is after all his bookkeeping.

Besides, it was not my business to overthrow heroes or create new ones. This play has no hero. It shows a chain of events. One can choose. Much that seems so shocking is to be found in any of the better histories and has long been known to scholars. If we, despite this, know only what corresponds to a certain briefing, and if this play by sticking to the facts can so turn our view of society upside down, this should arouse our mistrust. What kind of stories have we been told till now?